THE GOODNESS OF GOD

by
Dr. Edward L. Haygood

All Scripture quotations are from the *King James Version* of the Bible, unless otherwise indicated.

Scripture quotations marked NKJV are taken from *The New King James Version of the Bible*. Copyright © 1979, 1980, 1982, 1983, 1984 by Thomas Nelson, Inc. Publishers. Used by permission.

Scripture quotations marked NAS are taken from the *New American Standard Bible*. Copyright © The Lockman Foundation 1960, 1962, 1963, 1968, 1971, 1972, 1973, 1975, 1977. Used by permission.

Greek and Hebrew definitions are based on English transliterations listed in *Strong's Exhaustive Concordance of the Bible*, by Hendrickson Publishers, and William Wilson's *Old Testament Word Studies Lexicon and Concordance*, by Kregel Publication.

The Goodness of God
ISBN 0-89274-977-6
Copyright © 1996 by
Dr. Edward L. Haygood
Agape Christian Fellowship
12700 South Main Street
Los Angeles, California 90061

Published by Harrison House, Inc.
P.O. Box 35035
Tulsa, Oklahoma 74153

All rights reserved. Written permission must be secured from the publisher to use or reproduce any part of this book, except for brief quotations in critical reviews or articles. Printed in the United States of America.

CONTENTS

Introduction 5
1 O Taste and See! 7
2 Goodness: God's First Known Attribute 25
3 Only God Is Good 39
4 How Good Is God? 49
5 Trusting in God's Goodness 73
6 God Is Good to All 87
7 Thanksgiving and the Goodness of God. 103
Epilogue 124

INTRODUCTION

When I began this study on the goodness of God, I was amazed to see all the scriptures in which God admonishes us to be aware of His goodness. I had read these scriptures over and over again without ever really looking at them. I just went on shouting "Hallelujah" and didn't realize that God was telling me something that would be beneficial to my life. I just never thought about it before.

As I continued to study, I discovered something wonderful! God is good! This book is a mini-exegesis to establish that fact. In order to understand God's goodness more clearly, we will study Psalm 34:8, *O taste and see that the Lord is good: blessed is the man that trusteth in him.*

We will also look at Psalm 34:7,9, and 10, as well as many other scriptures, in order to enhance Psalm 34:8 and bring out more of its power.

However, I would not want to become involved in this study without first asking for the Lord's direction, counsel, and guidance:

Father, as we prepare our hearts now for the study of Your Word, we ask that Your Spirit guide us as the Word goes forth in power and authority to accomplish that for which it was sent. Father, thank You for the Greater One who lives within us. In Your name, I pray that the Holy Spirit, who is the convicter and convincer and persuader of the truth, will reveal the truth about Your amazing goodness to every reader. We give You the praise and glory for this, in Jesus' name. Amen.

Chapter 1

O Taste and See!

O taste and see that the Lord is good: blessed is the man that trusteth in him.
—Psalm 34:8

Psalm 34:8 is a praise from David. In this verse, David confides that he has just discovered something he wants us to learn also. He has discovered that God is good! Like David, we must also discover this particular truth to enhance our lives and Christian walk with the Lord. We need to know without a doubt and be totally convinced and persuaded of this truth: GOD IS GOOD!

Sometimes it's helpful to sense the biblical environment at the time the scripture was written. It is particularly helpful to understand what the writer was experiencing, or had recently experienced, at the time he wrote.

In Psalm 34, David was praising and worshipping God, reflecting on all the Lord's help in times of extreme difficulty. At the same time, he was praying for continued deliverance in times of trouble. We need to get as close to that setting as we can and share as much as possible what David experienced in order to make a proper application of Psalm 34:8. Let's look at verse 7 in order to establish the environment: *The angel of the Lord encampeth round about them that fear him, and delivereth them.*

You might not see the relationship between verse 8—*O taste and see*—and verse 7—*the angel of the Lord* who is, in the Hebrew language, the *Malak Yahweh*. But these verses are very much related.

Now, who is this *Malak Yahweh?* Who is this angel of the Lord? He is the One who encamped around and about David and who encamps around and about us today. *As captain of the host of the Lord am I now come. And Joshua fell on his face to the earth, and did worship, and said unto him, What saith my lord unto his servant?* (Joshua 5:14.) As in verse 7, this makes reference to the pre-incarnate Christ who, I believe, is *the angel of the Lord*. This messenger of Jehovah is none other than Jesus Christ Himself, the epitome and the essence of "God with us." He *encampeth round about them that fear him*—underline that word <u>fear</u> because we're also going to learn something about fear as we progress in this study.

This *Malak Yahweh* who encamps around and about us is none other than the captain of the host of the Lord! Because God—a Spirit—is not limited by space or time, He can be in front of us at the same time that He is behind us, and to the right and to the left of us. He can be "up" at the same time that He is "down." In other words, He has you and me covered in all directions, at all times. Now that is GOOD!

Our God Is a Sun and Shield

Psalm 84—my favorite Psalm—sheds more light on this aspect of being covered by God's goodness. *For the Lord God is a sun and shield: the Lord will give grace and glory: no good thing will he withhold from them that walk uprightly* (Psalm 84:11).

What good is the sun? Everybody knows the answer! The sun gives life to the entire galaxy. In fact, our galaxy would be dead without the sun. The sun also brings life and plenty. It causes everything to grow. No sun...no growth ...no plenty. So we must have the sun.

Just as the sun is out there producing for us the plenty and the bounty in the earth, so is God. He is like that. He is saying, "I want to produce within YOU the plenty and the bounty!" But not only is God like a sun, according to Psalm 84:11, He is like a shield.

What is a shield for? It's another type of covering, or protection. God's goodness is the covering that was always used in the Old Testament to protect His people on their way. On the way to Canaan, the Israelites found protection and provision. They had plenty to eat and they walked in safety from their enemies every step of the way, even when they complained against God. Even though they said, "We're tired of this bread from heaven! We want some meat," they were protected. God said, "You want meat? All right, I'll send you some meat!" And He gave them so much meat that it ran out of their noses! They grew tired of meat! That's how bountiful He is!

God is good! He is a sun and shield. He provides for us and protects us. That's how good He is!

What else does He do? He gives us His grace and glory. But here's the part I really like: *No good thing will he withhold from them that walk uprightly.* Now, He didn't say, "No good thing will I withhold from those who talk a lot of nonsense...or from those who make 150 confessions per day!" And I'm not saying, don't do that! What I am saying is that without fellowship with God, you'll get zero! That's what David wanted us to see.

We must first have the experience of tasting, then seeing the goodness of God. One experience produces the next experience. Salvation is an event that leads to a process which, in turn, leads to glorification. We all need to be able to look back on a specific event which marked our salvation, and it should be more than just signing a card! We must KNOW what we believe.

If you do not know the Lord in this personal way, let me shake you gently. Wake up! Do you really think that because you know with your intellect there is a God that you will one day go to heaven? Admit it! You're scared to death that if you dropped dead of a heart attack, you'd go to hell! And because you're scared, you already instinctively know that simply believing there is a God up there somewhere is not enough. You'd better have an experience with Him to back that up. You'd better *taste and see!*

Tasting and Seeing

We're going to get down to some heavy stuff now! *God is a Spirit* (John 4:24). God, being a Spirit, is not limited by space. He encamps around and about us. Not being limited by space, He can therefore furnish protection to cover us on every side. That's why we must go back to Psalm 34:8 in order to understand what David was writing to you and me—so we can *taste* and *see* how good God really is!

Most of us don't really understand God's goodness. His goodness is not based upon situations, circumstances, individuals, days, denominations, or what kind of Bible you're reading—*New King James*, *Old King James*, authorized, unauthorized, revised, or devised! These things don't have anything to do with who God is. We need to *taste and see* if we are ever to fully understand the goodness of God.

O Taste and See!

First Peter 2:1-3 says, *Wherefore laying aside all malice, and all guile, and hypocrisies, and envies, and all evil speakings, As newborn babes, desire the sincere milk of the word, that ye may grow thereby: If so be ye have* TASTED *that the Lord is gracious.* (Emphasis mine.)

I've seen a few newborn babes in my day, and I've noticed something about them when they're hungry. When newborn babes are hungry, that hunger is not their problem—it's YOUR problem! And you better come to their rescue, because they'll scream and yell until you do! When newborn babes want to eat, their whole body shakes. You think they'll never stop crying. You pick them up, you lay them down, you turn them around, you turn them over, you lay them on their backs, you turn them on their sides, you pick them up again, you lay them down again. You rock them. You squeeze them. You say, "Goochie, goochie!" You pull on their ears. You do all kinds of things. But the baby is trying to tell you, "Hey, give me something to eat! That's all I want!"

Peter says, *As newborn babes, desire the sincere milk of the word, that ye may grow.* The key word here is GROW! In order for us to grow and mature in the things of the Lord, there are many things we must know, and one of those things is the goodness of God. We're going to have to know that in order to *grow thereby.* Peter doesn't stop there, but adds: *If so be ye have tasted.* If you study the Greek, you'll find out that this is a fulfilled condition. Peter doesn't say, "If ye taste." He says, "Since you have tasted."

If one desires to be fed as a newborn babe desires milk, one will taste! And when we taste, we discover something and then move on to the next experience after tasting. We discover that *the Lord is gracious* (1 Peter 2:3).

When God speaks to nonbelievers through the Bible, He never tells them to taste. He tells them to *eat*. Check it out! Once a nonbeliever has eaten, he can begin to grow. So when God speaks of tasting, it is always in reference to a mature individual.

Spiritual tasting can be likened to physical tasting. Consider how you taste new foods. Sometimes you just take a little taste of something because you are predisposed psychologically to react negatively. You may, in that case, reject it simply because you *think* you might not like it. But how can you say, "I don't like it?" You haven't even tasted it yet! That's the way I was when I was a kid, especially when it came to eating spinach. I remember saying, "No, I don't like it!" I just knew I didn't like spinach, even though I wasn't sure why. I love to eat spinach now. Eat the Word! Eat it, for only then will you discover whether or not you like it. Once you eat it, the next thing you know, you will have developed a taste for it. In fact, you'll hardly be able to keep from tasting it again and again!

In much the same way as I developed a taste for spinach, God wants you first to eat, spiritually! Once you eat of His Word and the things of God, you'll know what it's all about. It will create in you a desire to taste it some more. *If so be ye have tasted* [to see] *that the Lord is gracious.*

Tasting Precedes Seeing

O taste and see that the Lord is good (Psalm 34:8). The first thing you must understand about the divine truth contained in this verse is the relationship between the words *taste* and *see*. Just as the order in which these words are used in this verse, tasting always comes *before* seeing. In God's economy, one must *taste* before one *sees*. *Taste*...and when you taste, you'll *see*! To *see* in this context implies that one receives knowledge and understanding.

David said, "Just taste, and you can see something that I saw. If you don't taste, you won't see it. Taste and see!" *Taste* and you'll *see!* Taste and you'll understand! You'll know...you'll experience all!

Tasting is a spiritual experience. Tasting precedes seeing, just as spiritual experience leads to spiritual perception, or knowledge. You must TASTE that spiritual experience in order to have the necessary spiritual perception, which is SEEING. Spiritual experience leads to spiritual perception.

People today don't seem to want to spend the time necessary to get spiritual experience. They want to get everything by the "fast-food" method. They want to perceive, but they don't want to take the time to gain the necessary experience! Spiritual perception, however, is just not possible without spiritual experience.

Two Groups of People

Spiritually speaking, there are two groups of people— the unregenerated and the converted. The unregenerated are not capable of comprehending God's goodness. Their sense of taste has been vitiated...corrupted. It's been spoiled. It's perverted. Sin is what they have a taste for. It's what they live on. It's what they try to find pleasure in, not realizing that Hebrews 11:25 says those *pleasures of sin* [are only] *for a season.* Therefore, they disdain the things of God. They can't taste them. They have no understanding of them.

Here's where the unregenerated person has a problem. He cannot begin to see how good God is because he does not have the taste for it. That's why God can do good things for an unregenerated person and he will not even discern that it is God doing the good. The unregenerated man, therefore, cannot know that God is good, or see the good that God is doing in his life. That's a dangerous position to be in!

That's why it is so important to be born again. Something happens on the inside when you are born again, and something happens to your sense of taste, too. You are suddenly able to begin to taste the things of God and to see things in an entirely different perspective. Remember what Hebrews 11:25 says: *The pleasures of sin* [are] *for a season.*

Then there is the converted group. These individuals have been given a new sense of taste. Thus, they are able to see, and to arrive at some spiritual experience. This experience should lead to a saving, experiential knowledge of the grace and goodness of Jesus Christ. There should then be an application of that goodness in daily life, because it is just no good to taste and see, if there is not the proper application of what one has learned.

That's a real problem for some of us. We often read the Word of God...we taste it and see. We even come up with some new information as a result. But we never take that third important step, which is *applying* that information. Somehow, we just think the information is going to be applied for us. We think it's going to just happen. No, it's only going to happen when we apply it. When we finally understand that, things are going to happen on our behalf. When we finally begin to apply the realities of the things we have discovered in our Christian walk, things will definitely happen!

Christianity is work! We may think it's pressing buttons...like some kind of computer religion! But it's nothing like that! It's the workman who is not ashamed (see 2 Timothy 2:15)—not the button-pusher—who will ultimately succeed! We just think we're going to press some button, say something, and presto—it's just going to start coming out in some format that will make things happen overnight! But the truth is that we won't get results unless we make an application of what we have learned.

*Taste...see...*then *apply* what you have learned! If you don't apply it, then all you will have had is a passing experience. You'll have had some Christian experience that has no application in your daily life whatsoever. Of course, you'll be better off than the sinner, but you still won't be where you ought to be in the Lord's kingdom.

Tasting Should not be Superficial

We must understand some things about spiritual tasting. First, it should not be superficial. The Christian experience should not be some casual thing. We must not say, "Just give me a little bit! I just want a little taste! Don't preach too long! Don't stay all day! Don't give me too much Bible!" Think about it! This is not some superficial thing!

Second, it is not something to be tasted only once. We must taste it more than once. When my mother did a lot of cooking years ago, she would taste some dishes four, five, six, maybe even seven times before she finally got it right. But some people think they're so good, all they have to do is taste the things of God one time, and suddenly they're a genius! Suddenly they're the apostle sent for this day! "Hey, I read one scripture! Now I'll go out and declare it to the world and save everybody!" But we can't base our Christian experience on a single taste. Spiritual tasting must be frequent and repeated.

In addition, we must understand what it means to "meditate" on the Word day and night. We in the western world don't understand the eastern concept of meditation. In the biblical sense, *to meditate* means "to eat, much like the cow chews its cud." Think about it: A cow can take fresh green grass and dried brown grass, chew it up, and bring forth white milk and creamy yellow butter. But she didn't produce those things from a single taste. That cow was out there in the field, chewing all day long...chewing, chewing, chewing! All of a sudden, the next morning, there is milk! That which was considered of no value—grass—has now become a perfect sustenance—milk! That which appeared to be nothing is now something nourishing! That's how good God is!

Tasting Is a Personal Experience

No one can taste the things of God for you. You must do it for yourself. Do you remember in the summertime when it was real hot—maybe 95 or 100 degrees—how sometimes you would get a real cold bottle of that red pop and tell yourself, "I think I'll just have a little taste"? You'd turn that bottle up, and before you knew it, it was almost gone! You drank it so fast, you could hardly breathe! But it was so good you just couldn't stop!

Well, that's how tasting the things of God should be to you. Tasting spiritually must be frequent and repeated, because that's how good it is. Let me say this though: You've got to taste it for yourself! Nobody can taste it for you, just as nobody could drink that bottle of red pop for you! If someone else drinks it, that red pop won't do a thing to quench your thirst!

In fact, when you see someone else drinking, it should make you all the more thirsty. "Hey, give me some of that!" You cannot ask them how it tastes and really know the taste yourself. You must do it for yourself if you are ever going to come to the realization that God is good.

David Understood God's Goodness

David was experienced in the goodness of God. He understood it and was desirous that we might also experience the goodness of God. Then we might come to know the things he knew about God's goodness.

Psalm 34:10 says, *But they that seek the Lord shall not want any good thing.* David was successful in many areas of his life because he was able to understand the goodness of God. He was able to taste and see how good God really is.

Let's go back to verse 9: *O fear the Lord, ye his saints: for there is no want to them that fear him.* In this verse, we have the call to fear Jehovah. David is saying, "As you taste and see, also *fear* [Jehovah] *the Lord, ye his saints."* I wondered why he said that, so I looked it up. As I did, I thought about Philippians 4:19: *But my God shall supply all your need according to his riches in glory by Christ Jesus.* Then I compared it to Psalm 34:9: *O fear the Lord, ye his saints: for there is no want to them that fear him.*

I realized that we know these scriptures and we quote them and make clichés out of them, reciting them redundantly. But we may not really realize what God requires. Just because we rehearse a verse does not necessarily mean that verse is a reality in our lives! It's much the same with God's goodness. We don't realize how good God is. We just talk about His goodness. We come away with some cliché about His goodness without really understanding the concept. But we're going to find out some things about God's goodness as we progress in this study! We're going to find out about the requirements God places on those who endeavor to *taste and see*. And one of those requirements is that we fear Him!

The Fear of God

Joshua 24:14 tells us how to fear Jehovah: *Now therefore fear the Lord, and serve him in sincerity and in truth: and put away the gods which your fathers served on the other side of the flood, and in Egypt; and serve ye the Lord.* Why did He say, *And serve him* [this God you fear] *in sincerity and truth?* Because in this verse God is saying, "When you learn to do that—and to put away the false gods—you will be truly serving the Lord."

Did you know that a person always takes on the nature and the attributes of the God he serves? If you serve a monkey-god, you'll act like a monkey. If you serve a renegade, you'll act like a renegade. But if you plan to serve the one true living God, you'd better put away those idol-gods. By serving God in sincerity and truth, you will take on His attributes. That's why the psalmist said, *Fear God.*

First Samuel 12:24 also has something to teach us about serving God with sincerity and truth. It says: *Only fear the Lord, and serve him in truth with all your heart.* We already know that God wants sincerity and truth, but now we see that this fear of the Lord involves service with sincerity, with truth, and with the whole heart.

I'm getting ready to drop something on you now, so fasten your seat belt and get ready to shout! Verse 24 continues: *For consider how great things he hath done for you.* That's right! Consider the good things He's done for you! The psalmist says, *O taste and see that the Lord is good: blessed is the man that trusteth in him. O fear the Lord, ye his saints.* As if that wasn't blessing enough, notice what he says next: *There is no want to them that fear him* (Psalm 34:8,9).

Fear Him how? In sincerity, and *in truth with all your heart:* [as you] *consider how great things he hath done for you* (1 Samuel 12:24).

Once you do that—once you come to that particular experience of tasting—this spiritual experience will lead to your increased spiritual perception and knowledge. You will learn *there is no want to them that fear him.* That's what verse 9 says!

But wait a minute! What about verse 10, which says, *The young lions do lack, and suffer hunger?* What about that? Read the rest of verse 10, *But they that seek the Lord shall not want any good thing.*

What About the Young Lions?

What a paradox! First David says there is no want. Then he says there IS want! But what appears to be a paradox really is not. You must understand what God wants you to see. He wants you to realize the importance of having fellowship with Him. Just as He says there is no want to them that fear Him—that is, those who serve Him with sincerity, truth, and their whole hearts—He will create a situation in the lives of those who are not doing this for their good, to get them into fellowship with Him.

God is saying, "If I just automatically throw out My goodness, you'll get to the place where you take it for granted. In fact, you'll even forget to praise Me for it. You'll forget to fear Me. You won't be sincere. You won't be walking in truth. You won't consider how good I am, or what great things I've done for you. You'll just say, 'Oh, I know God is going to do it for me, honey! I'm a great saint! God always does it! In fact, He's blessing me right now!'"

If you are that way, I'm warning you—God will create a lack so you will learn to appreciate how good He really is. I know you don't want to hear this, but *the young lions DO lack* (v. 10). Now, God is quick to let you know there is nothing wrong with a young lion. Unlike an old lion who can no longer catch his prey, that young lion is BAD! He's king of the forest.

While I've never observed a lion in its natural habitat—the jungle—I saw one once in the San Francisco Zoo. As I walked by his cage, that lion just jumped up on the bars and roared. And when I heard that bad boy roar...well, I've never heard anything like it! It felt like the ground was shaking. I said to myself, "Yes sir, king of the jungle!" That roar had let me know that if he got out, I'd had it! He was a young lion and he was still strong. He still had power in his step. Nevertheless, he did lack. Why?

Because he was unable to capture his own food. He was totally dependent upon someone else for his prey. God says, "I'm going to prevent the prey from coming by. I'm not going to hurt the lion. I'm just not going to send any little antelope by today."

The lion in the forest looks up about breakfast time, and no antelope comes by as usual. Pretty soon it will be noon and lunchtime. But the lion hasn't had his breakfast yet. Still no antelope. Now it's almost dinner time. He didn't have lunch and he didn't have breakfast, and by now he's suffering hunger. Now what? It's time to seek the Lord. It's time to enter into fellowship with God, because only He can provide the good things that young lion needs.

All of a sudden the lion looks up and along comes a little antelope tripping out of the bushes. And all of this has taken place in order that we might understand the goodness of God!

Psalm 34:10 is a good illustration of this: *The young lions do lack, and suffer hunger: but they that seek the Lord shall not want any good thing.* This is something we must all understand—that God, in His goodness, will create a need for spiritual experience in order for us to learn some important things about spiritual perception.

Who are the young lions mentioned in verse 10? *Young lions,* in this case, is a metaphor used to describe youth and strength. Even though these lions are young and strong...even though they can leap and run down their prey ...these young lions still sometimes suffer lack. Why? Because God is saying, "No matter how strong and agile you are, sometimes there will be no prey! Then what are you going to do?"

Young lions are strong, fast, quick, and have an acute sense of smell. They are healthy and capable of catching the prey. Even with all these excellent attributes, the prey evades the young lions when it's time to hunt for food. Because there is no prey available, they suffer lack and experience hunger. God is good, though, and His mercy endureth forever. He'll take care of those young lions when there is no food.

Picture those lions—up on their toes, ready to pounce and catch something...but there's nothing to catch! *The young lions do lack, and suffer hunger.* Why are they lacking? The young lions suffer hunger because the Lord wants each one of them to desire the things of God. There must still be the desire, like newborn babes, for the things of God, even when there is no prey!

Psalm 104:21 also makes mention of young lions: *The young lions roar after their prey, and seek their meat from God.* Lions who are suffering hunger obviously don't just decide to hold a "lion prayer meeting" to seek the help of God! Nevertheless, they are crying out to God by instinct. But God has created man to be greater than that. If the lion is being fed by the goodness of God by sheer instinct, how much more will God feed those who are willingly able to call upon His assistance! That's what God wants us to see!

It's not the old, beat-up lions who are having trouble catching their prey—it's the young lions, the ones who are strong enough to catch it for themselves. Even these young, strong, spry ones must depend upon God for their food and for their very survival. The bottom line is that God is the provider, even for the king of the jungle. *These wait all upon thee; that thou mayest give them their meat in due season* (Psalm 104:27). The lion doesn't eat until God tells him it's time to eat. Even the lion—king of the jungle—doesn't eat until God supplies his food.

This same principle can be applied to humans. Maybe we need to hunger and thirst after something righteous from time to time. Too often we just presumptuously think things are going to happen a certain way. Then, suddenly, we find ourselves lacking. We find ourselves in hunger.

Whenever we find ourselves lacking or in hunger, the first thing we must do is fellowship with God and seek Him. The Lord is good, but He might desire that we experience some things in order to see what we otherwise would have missed. He is saying, "Once you find out and get back in fellowship with Me, you'll discover the things I'm trying to teach you, and you'll find out that everything is good. It's GOOD!"

So God is letting us know that when we enter into His fellowship, we are also entering into His goodness. But the thing that really astounds me about God's goodness is that He is willing to share it with us! He is saying, "Once you find out how good I really am—that it is my essence...my being—I will share that goodness with you, My saints! I will share the essence that is unspeakable and unexplainable with you, and I will share it simply because you desire to seek Me and trust in Me!"

Why, then, is the fear of God so important? Because whoever fears the Lord—and that could be you as you read this book—*possesses everything in Him*! God is saying, "If you will come to Me with sincerity and truth, you can have what I possess!" Listen to what David said: *O fear the Lord...for there is no want to them that fear him.* What is God saying to us through David? Those who fear Me possess everything there is in Me!" That's heavy!

Why do those who fear the Lord possess all that is in Him? Because they become so identified with Him! Remember, a person takes on the qualities and attributes of his God!

So put away those other gods! They can't give you anything! They're dumb! They have nothing to offer. When you put away all other gods and fear the one true God, you'll find there is no want. Remember, Philippians 4:19 is still based on a condition, and that condition does not call for much flapping of your lips! The condition requires that you have a relationship with God.

It's not what you say, it's first how you relate to God ...and THEN what you say! You can say a lot of things that sound good spiritually, but if you have no relationship with God, you'll still get zero! God is saying, "Seek Me, and I'll give you everything I am. Reverence Me, and you can possess all that I am. And I am the essence of goodness!"

That's what God was saying to David in Psalm 34 ...and that's what He is still saying to us today!

Chapter 2

Goodness: God's First Known Attribute

When you were first saved—but before you had any spiritual insight—you probably picked up your Bible and started reading Genesis. After about the first three chapters, you probably put it back down and said, "Forget it!"

Most of us did that! And how many of us ever finished reading Genesis the first time through? We read some things but still didn't understand what the Holy Spirit was trying to say in Genesis. What was that? From the very beginning, God was saying, "The first thing I want you to know about Me is that I am good!" But we missed it!

I know I missed it. I related the book of Genesis to something very practical and never saw anything about God Himself. But throughout this book, God is saying over and over again, "I'm going to let you know how GOOD I am!"

Now just think about that for a minute. God made the earth and He put you on it. He didn't have to tell you it was good, because you had no other choice but to receive it as it is. Yet God keeps drawing your attention to the fact of His goodness. Why?

Goodness is God's first known attribute. Described in the book of Genesis, it is the first attribute revealed to us by God about Himself. Thus, it seems His goodness was one of the divine motives which moved God to create the world and everything in it, including mankind. He wanted to display His goodness!

God starts telling us right away in Genesis 1:4, that everything He is doing is good. He says, "I'm creating everything and you need to learn something—that My divine motive in creating everything was My goodness!" The goodness of God is the first attribute describing His creation.

The Goodness of Creation

And God saw the light, that it was good: and God divided the light from the darkness. And God called the light Day, and the darkness he called Night. And the evening and the morning were the first day (Genesis 1:4,5). God called the light GOOD! But He didn't say a thing about darkness. Why? Because He was looking only for that which is good to comment on.

And God called the dry land Earth; and the gathering together of the waters called he Seas: and God saw that it was good (v. 10). Again God emphasizes the goodness of His creation. If such goodness is revealed in God's creation, how much more should we see it revealed in His Person, because God's creation is simply the reflection, or impartation, of who He really is!

And the earth brought forth grass, and herb yielding seed after his kind, and the tree yielding fruit, whose seed was in itself, after his kind: and God saw that it was good (v. 12). In this verse, God is trying to tell us something. He has already talked about the light. He has already talked about the earth. Now, in verse 12, He tells us, *And the earth brought forth grass*...or vegetation and plants, and herbs, and trees—all bearing seed and yielding fruit after its kind.

God had just set up a system for you and me. And He called it good!

Some of you already know about this system. Once you find out about seeds and how things are designed to produce after themselves, you can indulge and sometimes even over-indulge! Just take a minute to reflect on the things God is producing for you! You'd better *taste* it! And don't ever forget that God is good. Everything He does is to let you know, "Hey—I'm good! Everything I make is good! Even those greens you ate for lunch are good."

Created for our Good

Why did God create this system of seed-bearing plants? I believe it was to teach us about His goodness. Through this system, every person on earth ought to be able to understand that God is good. We might even say God is dealing with all men on the basis of His goodness—not just believers, but all mankind. He wants us to know simply by observing the world around us and considering nature that He is good.

How could anyone serve another god? It's a slap in God's face, and sooner or later those who serve other gods will have to deal with that. One day God will say, "How could you do that? Didn't you see that everything I did was good? I did it all for you because I am intrinsically good within Myself. The problem is not with Me—it's with you! You just need to know how GOOD I am! I'm a GOOD God!"

Now let's look at Genesis 1:16-18: *And God made two great lights; the greater light to rule the day, and the lesser light to rule the night: he made the stars also. And God set them in the firmament of the heaven to give light upon the earth. And to rule over the day and over the night, and to divide the light from the darkness: and God saw that it was good.* Notice—God SAW that it was good! Isn't that interesting! Why didn't He just say, "God KNEW that it was good?" I mean, He could have said that! But instead, He chose the word *saw.* He was saying to you and me, "Wake up! Look around! Use your senses to learn something!"

God didn't need to see His creation. He already knew everything about it. He could have said, "Hey, I made it that way! It's not for Me to see—it's for you to see!" *And God created great whales, and every living creature that moveth, which the waters brought forth abundantly, after their kind, and every winged fowl after his kind: and God saw that it was good* (v. 21). Even whales are good! Now, I don't get out there and swim with those big guys, but God said, "It's good!" So I'll admire them from the shore. But God said He created the whales, along with every other living creature, and called them all good.

This is not some fairy tale. We're building something real here. Just look at verse 25: *And God made the beast of the earth after his kind, and cattle after their kind, and every thing that creepeth upon the earth after his kind: and God saw that it was good.* Again, every animal in creation is called GOOD.

Full of God's Goodness

Now let's look at Psalm 33 and we'll begin to see the results of this display of God's goodness. *Sing unto him a new song; play skilfully with a loud noise. For the word of the Lord is right; and all his works are done in truth. He loveth righteousness and judgment* [now, watch what He says here]*: the earth is full of the goodness of the Lord* (vv. 3-5). Right in the middle of Psalm 33, the psalmist

Goodness: God's First Known Attribute

stops to sing the praises of God and to tell us that the earth is full—FULL—of the goodness of God!

Hey, that's the first thing God wants us to know about Him! He created all these good things because of truth. He did all His works in truth, as the psalmist said, and all the earth is full of His goodness.

Just start thinking about that. Everything you have is because of the goodness of God. It's not because you're so great or because you won the contest. It's not even because you were born into a certain family. It's because of God's goodness.

We've just learned that the earth is full of God's goodness. Now the psalmist proceeds to reaffirm what we saw in Genesis 1. *By the word of the Lord were the heavens made; and all the host of them by the breath of his mouth* (Psalm 33:6). Now, God is good, and He just transposed that goodness throughout His creation. He just breathed that goodness throughout the earth! He just said, "BE!" And it was! And afterwards He saw it and said, "It's GOOD! It's VERY GOOD!" The Lord said, "I saw that it was good, but you'd better look and find out that it's good, also."

He gathereth the waters of the sea together as an heap: he layeth up the depth in storehouses (v. 7). Now, why do you have a storehouse? Because you have more than you actually need. Storehouses! *Let all the earth fear the Lord: let all the inhabitants of the world stand in awe of him. For he spake, and it was done; he commanded, and it stood fast* (vv. 8,9). There it is! The psalmist said, "He's an awesome God, and because He is, you'd better stand in awe of Him!" Why? Because He spoke and it was done! What was done? Good was done! He just spoke, and good was done! And we are to stand in awe!

Verse 9 is saying something else: *He commanded, and it stood fast.* That word *fast* actually means "firm." *He commanded, and it stood firm.* He said the earth is full of His goodness, and it's not going away. There's enough for everybody, and even enough for those who misuse it. Goodness is still in abundant supply. It stands firm!

You'll never hear, "We're running out of this and we're running out of that!" Not in God's kingdom. You may not be able to see it, but it's just because you don't know where it is.

Do you know how the Hearst family made their fortune? Some folks think the Hearsts made their fortune in newspapers, but that's not so. Granddaddy Hearst struck gold in California! That gold was hidden, but God revealed it to him! He got in on that gold. Later he spent some of his money in newspapers.

Regardless of what folks say about running out of things on earth, there is still an abundant supply, if people just know where to look. Remember, the earth is FULL of God's goodness! So you can see why the prophets Elijah and Elisha could, in faith, make such bold demands upon God. If they found the cruse of oil empty, they reminded God, "But You said the earth is FULL of your goodness!" In the story of the poor widow woman (1 Kings 17:10-16), the cruse of oil did not run dry. Elijah prayed on her behalf and God multiplied the oil and the meal. There was a miraculous supply that not only provided for her immediate needs, but for her future needs as well. Why did God move so miraculously for the widow woman? Because He's good!

God Requires our Praise

Psalm 107:1,2 says, *O give thanks unto the Lord, for he is good: for his mercy endureth for ever. Let the redeemed of the Lord say so, whom he hath redeemed from the hand of the enemy.* The psalmist is telling us that we have a responsibility to always give God praise for His goodness. *O give thanks unto the Lord, for he is good...Let the redeemed of the Lord say so!* We, the redeemed of the Lord, are the ones who have tasted of His goodness. We have eaten of the goodness of God. Therefore, we are the ones who must "say so" as we offer up our praises to God.

Verse 3 continues, *And gathered them out of the lands, from the east, and from the west, from the north, and from the south.* God is in the business of gathering folks. We have been gathered by Him that we might fall into four basic categories, according to Psalm 107. In each instance, we see the goodness of God revealed in His deliverance of the people. These groups are:

- The plight of the man on his journey by land (vv. 4-9).
- The plight of the prisoner enslaved (vv. 10-16).
- The plight of the one who is sick (vv. 17-22).
- The plight of the sea voyager in a storm (vv. 23-32).

In Psalm 107, God reveals His divine goodness to the tired and bewildered traveler. The Bible calls men "pilgrims." We are all sojourners. We are travelers. None of us even has a place to lay our head unless God provides one. We had better learn that, instead of talking about our fine houses and other possessions! We don't have anything apart from God.

In this Psalm, God also reveals His goodness to the enslaved captive. Just think about the many things that enslave us and make us captive, but God steps in and sets us free again and again.

God's goodness is revealed to the sick and dying. Some of you may have been so sick that God just stepped right in there and brought you back to life, without you even going to a doctor.

Finally, God reveals His goodness to those in the midst of a storm. In many situations that overwhelm us, we barely think to cry anything but, "Help!" And still God navigates us right into peaceful waters.

The Journey by Land
They wandered in the wilderness in a solitary way; they found no city to dwell in. Hungry and thirsty, their soul fainted in them. Then they cried unto the Lord in their trouble, and he delivered them out of their distresses. And he led them forth by the right way, that they might go to a city of habitation. Oh that men would praise the Lord for his goodness, and for his wonderful works to the children of men! For he satisfieth the longing soul, and filleth the hungry soul with goodness (Psalm 107:4-9).

A man stopped me the other day and said, "Pastor, there's a lot of distress going on today. It's all over!"

I replied, "Distress is common to man. But I'm here to tell you that God says there is deliverance in distresses." Verse 7 says, *And he led them forth by the right way, that they might go to a city of habitation.* He helped them. When they were hungry and thirsty, in distress, homeless, He helped them. I mean, these people were in bad shape!

Just because you have a house today does not mean that next week you're going to have one. I'm sure a lot of those folks out there in the wilderness never dreamed they'd ever be in such a helpless position. But God will show His goodness to you—no matter how distressing the circumstances—when you taste and see His goodness and praise Him for it.

I like what verse 8 says: *Oh that men would praise the Lord for his goodness, and for his wonderful works to the children of men!* Notice in these verses that each display of God's goodness caused praise to issue forth from the psalmist. God's goodness caused a response to spring forth from those who were the recipients of His goodness. They were praising God for His good work! Therefore, it appears to me that even in trouble—and in the journey of man, there will be trouble—there is a dimension reserved for God's goodness. Not even trouble can stop the goodness of God.

The Prisoner Enslaved

Although the description of the plight of the prisoner enslaved actually begins in verse 10, we must back up to include verse 9 for a better understanding of its meaning. *For he satisfieth the longing soul, and filleth the hungry soul with goodness. Such as sit in darkness and in the shadow of death, being bound in affliction and iron; Because they rebelled against the words of God, and contemned the counsel of the most High: Therefore he brought down their heart with labour; they fell down, and there was none to help. Then they cried unto the Lord in their trouble, and he saved them out of their distresses. He brought them out of darkness and the shadow of death, and brake their bands in sunder. Oh that men would praise the Lord for his goodness, and for his wonderful works to the children of men! For he hath broken the gates of brass, and cut the bars of iron in sunder* (Psalm 107:9-16).

"Oh, that men would praise Me!" Listen! He's telling you that the problem is, people won't praise Him. Then they find themselves in some terrible situation and they begin to cry out to God. Why do they wind up in that situation? Because they refused to praise God. He is pleading with all people, "Please, won't you just praise Me? You're the one in hunger...you're the one in distress...you're the one without a habitation! O, that men would praise Me!"

Just sense the heart of God, if you can, and you will sense that He wants to help mankind. But so often people turn their noses up at God and exempt themselves from Him. I can just hear God saying, *Oh that men would praise the Lord for his goodness, and for his wonderful works to the children of men* (v. 15)! Who is the recipient of His goodness? The children of men! He did not say He would do the same with His grace...just His goodness. He wants to display His goodness to the children of men—all of them!

Now, you might say, "Well, I've never been a prisoner!" Oh, yes you have! Anyone without Christ is bound in some type of bond that is greater than iron. So there is a personal application for everyone here.

The One who Is Sick

Fools, because of their transgression, and because of their iniquities, are afflicted. Their soul abhorreth all manner of meat; and they draw near unto the gates of death. Then they cry unto the Lord in their trouble, and he saveth them out of their distresses. He sent his word, and healed them, and delivered them from their destructions. Oh that men would praise the Lord for his goodness, and for his wonderful works to the children of men! And let them sacrifice the sacrifices of thanksgiving, and declare his works with rejoicing (Psalm 107:17-22).

Folks are released from the hospital every day and never thank God. They don't recognize the hand of God gave their doctor the wisdom and skill to do what was necessary to get them well. They send their doctors letters and cakes, yet they never once stand up and say, "Thank You, God! I was sinking down to the gates of death and You healed me!"

I had a little scratchy throat the other day. I decided to offer up my throat to the Lord, and He came down with the healing. Psalm 107:20,21 says, *He sent his word, and healed them, and delivered them from their destructions.* Some people aren't even saved, yet they have experienced God's healing many times. *Oh that men would praise the Lord for his goodness, and for his wonderful works to the children of men!*

I remember once thinking that Mama healed me. I didn't praise God. Besides, I knew that when Mama was concocting some home remedy, she was probably praying, "Lord, I don't know what this is, but I ask You to heal my boy when I put this mustard plaster on his chest. Heal him! Deliver him from his distresses and heal his body. Send Your Word!"

I know many of you have been there too. Most of you are still scared to go to an institution with all those guys in white coats running around, and you don't even trust God! You say, "I think I'll just go get some kind of remedy!" And you even wait until the last minute before you do that! If the Holy Spirit leads you to see a doctor, pray for him and praise God for giving him the answer to your problem. But whether or not you see a doctor—trust God! He's the Healer!

The Sea Voyager in a Storm

They that go down to the sea in ships, that do business in great waters; These see the works of the Lord, and his wonders in the deep. For he commandeth, and raiseth the stormy wind, which lifteth up the waves thereof. They mount up to the heaven, they go down again to the depths: their soul is melted because of trouble. They reel to and fro, and stagger like a drunken man, and are at their wit's end (Psalm 107:23-27).

Have you ever been at your wit's end? Have the storms of life ever taken you there? I've been there! God is not necessarily saying you have to be out in the middle of the Pacific Ocean in order to apply this passage of text. It could apply to any of us who are being tossed about by the winds and the waves of life. The storms of life will take you to your wit's end. You'll wind up at the point that you can't even think straight. What's happening? It's so stormy where you are, that you just give up thinking! You're at your wit's end. Your mind just goes blank. But there is something you can do: *Then they cry unto the Lord in their trouble, and he bringeth them out of their distresses. He maketh the storm a calm, so that the waves thereof are still. Then are they glad because they be quiet; so he bringeth them unto their desired haven. Oh that men would praise the Lord for his goodness, and for his wonderful works to the children of men!* (Psalm 107:28-31.)

Do you know what your prayer life will wind up being like during these times? "God...You've been so good! Thank You! Thank You! Hallelujah! Gracias!" You'll be trying to say "thank you" every way you know how to say it. Just looking back over your day, or even over the last few moments, you'll be able to see how good God is.

Notice that the goodness of God manifests itself in Psalm 107 in deliverance, and not just ordinary, run-of-the-mill deliverance. God can perform that kind of deliverance too. But the deliverance described in this Psalm is not just ordinary—it's tremendous! God is telling you, "I can give you the ordinary. I can give you the commonplace. But I can also give you things that are not run-of-the-mill. In fact, it doesn't matter what kind of trials come your way because I'm there!" Throughout the Bible, God performed these tremendous deliverances—in the wilderness, in Egyptian captivity, in the fiery furnace, in the lion's den.

And He did it all simply because He is good!

Chapter 3

Only God Is Good

I was working out at the gym recently when a woman approached me and told me she had heard me speak on a radio talk show. Then she asked, "Why do bad things happen to good people?"

Now, that's a good question. That's actually a theological question that most of us have asked from time to time, and one that may not even have an answer.

I answered the woman by saying, "You know, that's really not the issue. The issue is this: Only One is good, and that's God. Man is not good. In fact, there is no good in any of us. So whatever happens to man is not the issue, since there are no 'good' men. Only God is good. And since we are not good within ourselves, the only goodness we will ever have is the goodness that comes from God."

I explained to her that mankind basically seeks after evil, and God understands that. So whatever we might consider to be morally good or socially good has no bearing on the goodness of God, because none of us is good, no, not one! It is, therefore, of no consequence when we compare ourselves in terms of moral goodness to someone else because that only has to do with the order of society. It has nothing to do with God's standard of goodness, which only He possesses. She stood there and looked at me for a minute with her mouth wide open. Then she said, "Boy, you just answered the whole question!"

Hey, she caught me at the right time! If I had not just been studying about the goodness of God, I would have had no answer. I would have probably just replied, "Well, I don't know! I don't know why God is good to some folks and not to others!"

However, I do know this: What you and I call "good" is not GOOD! I mean, just because we have a social concept of goodness does not mean that we are under some um-brel-la of protection so that no evil can come into our lives. Why? Because God's concept of goodness is ABSOLUTE goodness—goodness above all that we can even conceive of, let alone understand.

We have already seen that the Psalmist David told us to *taste and see that the Lord is good* (Psalm 34:8). He also tells us that not everyone has the ability to *taste and see!* If we look at Psalm 34:8 from the superficial standpoint, we'll miss this. The psalmist is saying that even for those who *taste,* not everyone will *see.* He is saying that only those believers who have received the like nature of the Lord will be able to *taste and see.*

Then, after tasting and seeing, one must discern how good the Lord is! So we really don't need to get into any arguments or dissertations about why bad things happen to "good" people!

That is really not the issue at all. The issue is that God is good, regardless of the circumstances. And His goodness is not based upon what is happening to certain groups of people. I don't know why folks are starving in Africa. I don't understand that! But that doesn't mean God isn't good! The fact that starvation and killing exist in the world tells me more about the evil and corruption of man than about why God has allowed these things to occur.

Why do we keep putting God in the position of responsibility for all the evil in the world? In fact, it is man who causes bad things to happen to "good" people! But we can only understand that when we have fully come to realize that God is good. And we can only do that as we learn to *taste and see.* Just as God has given us a list of the benefits of His goodness, He has also told us something about Himself: "I'm faithful! I'm faithful to perform every one of those benefits to you! My goodness will endure!"

Even when mankind ascribes the bad things that are happening in this world to God, that doesn't hinder God's ability to be good. The psalmist tells us to *taste and see*—and only believers, who have the ability to discern God's goodness, will be able to understand it.

The "Goodness" of Man

Nevertheless, somewhere along the line, mankind has developed the idea of the "goodness of man." We hear it said all the time, in fact: "He's a 'good' man" or "She's a 'good' woman!" In fact, we all have that idea. We boast about it. Our friends and neighbors pump us up by telling us how "good" we are! "You're so good, you can do anything you want to! Nobody can stop you except yourself. That's how good you are!"

Now, I'm not saying that some of this is not good, if we keep it in the proper perspective. We need just enough of this kind of confidence to keep us going in the natural realm. But Jesus had something to say about the goodness of man. And in order to understand it, we need to consider the story of the rich young ruler.

> *And, behold, one came and said unto him, Good Master, what good thing shall I do, that I may have eternal life? And he said unto him, Why callest thou me good? there is none good but one, that is, God: but if thou wilt enter into life, keep the commandments. He saith unto him, Which? Jesus said, Thou shalt do no murder, Thou shalt not commit adultery, Thou shalt not steal, Thou shalt not bear false witness, Honour thy father and thy mother: and, Thou shalt love thy neighbour as thyself. The young man saith unto him, All these things have I kept from my youth up: what lack I yet? Jesus said unto him, If thou wilt be perfect, go and sell that thou hast, and give to the poor, and thou shalt have treasure in heaven: and come and follow me. But when the young man heard that saying, he went away sorrowful: for he had great possessions. Then said Jesus unto his disciples, Verily I say unto you, That a rich man shall hardly enter into the kingdom of heaven. And again I say unto you, It is easier for a camel to go through the eye of a needle, than for a rich man to enter into the kingdom of God. When his disciples heard it, they were exceedingly amazed, saying, Who then can be saved? But Jesus beheld them, and said unto them, With men this is impossible; but with God all things are possible* (Matthew 19:16-26).

Notice that the story begins with, *And, behold....* Now, when Jesus says, "Behold," He wants you to really look intently at the story that follows. *Behold* means "to look with expectancy, to look with anticipation, to look with hope." What are we to *behold* about this story? We are introduced to a man who came to Jesus. He came the right way, but he blew it just as some of us have blown it. He came saying, "Good Master." And that's right, because we know God is essentially good. And coming to Jesus with the salute, "Good Master," was right. But then he got off track, by asking, "What good thing shall I do?"

Doing Good Is not the Key

Anyone who is patting himself on the back for his goodness probably hasn't heard that good folks go to hell! Hello! Let me repeat—GOOD FOLKS GO TO HELL! Doing good won't get you into heaven! Now, we all want to do good. But this man had an angle: *Good Master, what good thing shall I do, that I may have eternal life?*

Jesus is going to summarize this for him. He's really going to tell him! "Just hook up with the Good Master, and then you'll have eternal life!" He was saying to the rich young ruler, "Nothing you can do will purchase eternal life. There is no good thing you can do! The only thing you have to do is hook up with Me!"

But when Jesus began to explain it, the young man said, "No way!"

Jesus was saying, "Wake up, young man! You ask what good thing you can do to receive eternal life, and then you call Me *good*. Receive Me and you will have done all the good you can do to inherit eternal life!" But this young man was obviously seeking to do some *things,* to have some "hands-on" experience to work himself into heaven.

There are churches throughout the world today that are designed to have folks do something because they promote the idea that you've got to help God get you into the kingdom. And that is as far off base as it can be! You can't do anything!

The Bible tells us there is no good thing we can do to earn a place in heaven. In fact, the Bible even tells us there is nothing about you and me that is good! (Matthew 19:17.)

As you progress in this study, you're going to learn that the word *good* does not apply to man or mankind. It applies only to God. Do you want something good? Then receive God, because only He is essentially good. Only He is solely good. And if you go to heaven, it will be because of His goodness, not yours.

Jesus asked the rich young man, *Why callest thou me good?* Then He said, "I'm going to tell you something, young man. None of us is good! Now, in your opinion, you might think you're good, but you are deceived!" The truth contained in this story is so vital that Jesus gave it to us three times—in the gospels of Matthew, Mark, and Luke—in order to fulfill the Mosaic Law. Jesus wanted us to really understand that there is none good but One!

The young man probably said, "Well, what one is that?" And Jesus might have said, "Well, I'm glad you asked! That's God, God Himself!"

How, then, can God communicate that goodness to us?

A Process of Diffusion

When I was taking chemistry, I learned about the process of diffusion. I learned that things can move from a point of higher concentration to a point of lower concentration. When we performed certain experiments to illustrate that law, we said, "The gases have diffused." In much the same way, God can take that higher goodness—His own higher concentration of goodness—and communicate it down to us by the process of diffusion. Thus, we who are lower are capable of experiencing that which is high.

In other words, a superior God who is essentially good will give you His goodness and allow you to operate in it, even though He says, "There is none good, no, not one!"

But that One who is good is able to diffuse that goodness downward. In that case, you'd better taste it, and you'd better find out something about it, because God says, "I require goodness, but the goodness I require is not present in you! It has to be diffused downward to you from Me!"

Why does God give this goodness to us? I still don't understand why God is so willing to share His nature with us! If I were God, I'd probably show the back of my hand to some folks on a consistent basis. But God doesn't do that simply because of His benevolent nature. We must understand God from His perspective—not ours—if we are to understand this process of diffusing His goodness down to us. If we don't see it from God's perspective, it will just confuse us.

Let's look at Jeremiah 29:10,11: *For thus saith the Lord, That after seventy years be accomplished at Babylon I will visit you, and perform my good word toward you, in causing you to return to this place. For I know the thoughts that I think toward you, saith the Lord, thoughts of peace, and not of evil, to give you an expected end.*

Remember, God is infinitely good! If He ever showed His goodness toward someone else, He is still able to show that same goodness today. If God was able to demonstrate His goodness as far back as the Babylonian empire, that same God who does not change is able to make His goodness available to us today. In Jeremiah 29:10,11, He is saying: "I'm going to show you some goodness! After seventy years are accomplished at Babylon, I will visit you and perform my good word toward you. I'm going to take you out of Babylonian captivity. I'm going to change your circumstances! Seventy years may have passed, but don't forget that I'm still God, and I am able to turn that thing around!" He's sharing His goodness! Can you see it? He is communicating it! He is diffusively giving it to us. He is taking His goodness from a high level and getting it right down to where we live.

For I know the thoughts that I think toward you (v. 11). Now, these were folks who had turned their backs on God to such an extent that He could no longer deal with them. He said, "Because you have turned your backs on Me so many times, I sent all kinds of people to you—judges, prophets, kings. I've been telling you and telling you, and you still couldn't get it right." That's why the people went into Babylonian captivity—to get what I call the "gold cure!" They had been making idols out of gold.

Some people, in fact, need the "gold cure" today! It's called "money" now, but there are many people who can't give God any time because they're too hung up on money. They're so hung up on it they work three or four jobs to obtain it. They don't have time to read and study, and they can't take time to go to church. They don't even have time to pray.

These people had better get cured, because if they don't cure themselves, God will send them to a place where He'll cure them...just like the people who were sent to Babylon. He sent them down there and said, "I'm going to put so many idol-gods in front of you that every time you look around, you'll see an idol-god!" And do you know something? It worked! To this day, Jews are not idolaters! Some may not believe in God, but they will not set up an idol figure and worship it instead. Why? Because those

Babylonians beat their heads to death with idol-gods for seventy years.

Then God said, "After you learn that you can have no other gods before Me, I'll set you free of that!" Why did He do it? *For I know the thoughts that I think toward you, saith the Lord, thoughts of peace, and not of evil, to give you an expected end* (Jeremiah 29:11). That's good!

God Is Thinking About You

You ought to mark that verse! I've got mine underlined with red and black! Whatever color of ink you choose, you should mark Jeremiah 29:11. It says God is thinking about you. The Jews who were sent into Babylonian captivity for seventy years had never once left the thoughts of God! That's how good He is! They may have forgotten about Him, but He never forgot about them. Finally He said, "One day I'm going to come—after seventy years—and I'm going to extend My hand to you again. I'm going to show you how really good I am! I'm going to set you free and return you to your homeland. Then I'm going to demonstrate some things to you because I like you so well! I'm going to put you back into your own land, and I'm going to give you an expectation and a hope! I'm going to give you a bright future!"

Listen to the *New King James* translation of Jeremiah 29:11: *For I know the thoughts that I think toward you, says the Lord, thoughts of peace and not of evil, to give you a future and a hope.* Now I like that! Although there are many translations, I would like to share only one more—the *New American Standard Version*. It says, *"For I know the plans that I have for you,"* declares the Lord, *"plans for welfare and not for calamity to give you a future and a hope."*

How unfortunate that the rich young ruler did not experience the goodness of God! For all that is contained in God's goodness could have been his, if only he had been able to see that he himself possessed no good thing, but Jesus epitomized all that is good. He would have poured His goodness into the life of the rich young ruler, but the young man could not receive it. The good news today is that all of His marvelous goodness is available to us as we continue to seek His will in our lives.

Chapter 4
How Good Is God?

Has anyone ever asked you: *How good is God?* What would you say if someone asked you that question today? Well, by the time you've finished this study, you'll have enough fresh insight into the goodness of God to be able to discuss the topic for hours!

I believe you will discover, as I did, the depth of God's goodness, as well as its broad application within our daily lives.

What did I discover as I conducted my research into God's goodness? I learned that He is:

- essentially good
- infinitely good
- the essence of goodness
- perfectly good
- immutably good
- ineffably good
- indescribably good
- inarticulately good
- solely good

But I'm not always confident with the English language. I just don't feel quite good about saying, "God is good," and stopping there. After all, what does that really tell me? So the Lord led me to a book that contained the Greek translation of the word, *good*. I discovered that there are several words for *goodness*. But we will look at only three of them. We will also study the Hebrew text to get an even better idea of just how good God really is.

Greek Words for "Good"

First let's look at the Greek word, *agathos*. It describes that which, being good in its character or constitution, is beneficial in its effect. It's no good for someone to have a character and a constitution that are good if they don't do any good with those attributes. That goodness must be of some benefit. It must be beneficial!

Psalm 104:28b is a good example of *agathos, Thou openest thine hand, they are filled with good.* God is saying, "I am good in both My character and My constitution, and because of that, I will open My hand." When someone opens his hand to you, you may have all that is contained in that extended hand. God is saying, "Now in My *agathos* goodness—which describes My character and My constitution—I will show you the beneficial effects of that goodness. I'll take My character and My constitution and I'll extend it to you in My outstretched, open hand. Then verse 28b says, *They are filled with good.*

God is saying, "I want to fill you with My goodness!" If only the rich young ruler had been able to see that! He could have had all that good, but he refused to sell his possessions because he thought he would lose it all. But God was saying, "If only you had sold that stuff, I would have extended My hand to you and I would have filled you with My goodness—the kind of goodness you had never had before!" But the man was very rich, and said, "I've got to stay with this gold, baby!" He had no idea that the gold market was uncertain and would fluctuate!

Hey, even gold may be no good some day! The Bible says that not even gold will be reliable forever. But the goodness of God is forever! He is INFINITELY good! Do you see why Jesus didn't run after the rich young ruler? He extended His goodness to him, but the young man walked away. Jesus let him go. And He went right on to the next subject.

Now let's look at Philemon 1:14: *But without thy mind would I do nothing; that thy benefit* [agathos] *should not be as it were of necessity, but willingly.* What is Paul saying in his letter to Philemon? That God's goodness and His good will come unto us as God's benefit. Remember, the word used here is *agathos*—"that which is beneficial." So God's goodness is of benefit.

Bless the Lord, O my soul: and all that is within me, bless his holy name. Bless the Lord, O my soul, and forget not all his benefits: Who forgiveth all thine iniquities; who healeth all thy diseases; Who redeemeth thy life from destruction; who crowneth thee with lovingkindness and tender mercies; Who satisfieth thy mouth with good things; so that thy youth is renewed like the eagle's (Psalm 103:1-5).

You ought to kick off your shoes sometimes and just sit back and thank God for how good He is! That's what David did in Psalm 103. *Bless the Lord, O my soul, and forget not all his benefits!* That's His *agathos*, His goodness that is present to deliver...His goodness that encamps around you everywhere you go. He forgives your iniquities. He heals you. He redeems your life from destruction. He crowns your life with love and kindness and with tender mercies. He satisfies your mouth with good things. He even renews your youth like the eagle's. All these are

The Goodness of God

attributes of God's goodness. And you can only get that kind of goodness one way—it only comes from God!

There's another quality of the word *good* from the Greek word *agathosune,* which stems from *agathos,* and means "goodness signifying moral quality." This word is used to describe born-again, regenerated people—those who are new creatures in Christ.

The word *agathosune* is used in Romans 15:14: *And I myself also am persuaded of you, my brethren, that ye also are full of goodness* [agathosune], *filled with all knowledge, able also to admonish one another.*

Agathosune is used again in this particular manner in Galatians 5:22,23: *But the fruit of the Spirit is love, joy, peace, longsuffering, gentleness, goodness* [agathosune]*, faith, meekness, temperance: against such there is no law.* Remember, *agathosune* is a quality that God wishes to apply to you as a regenerated person. You are to have this quality of moral goodness if you are, indeed, born of the Spirit. He wants you to be full of moral goodness—this *agathosune*—that is part of the fruit of the Spirit.

In fact, the only way the world can really know we are filled with the Spirit is by the evidence of the "fruit of the Spirit" in our lives, as described in Galatians, chapter 5. These are:

- love
- joy
- peace
- longsuffering
- gentleness
- goodness *(agathosune)*
- faith

- meekness
- temperance

Verse 23 goes on to say, *Against such there is no law.* There is no law to legislate moral quality. You cannot legislate it! It must come from God.

This type of *agathosune* goodness is again mentioned in Ephesians 5:9: *(For the fruit of the Spirit is in all goodness* [agathosune] *and righteousness and truth).* Again it applies to regenerated people! We can see this same thing again in 2 Thessalonians 1:11: *Wherefore also we pray always for you, that our God would count you worthy of this calling, and fulfil all the good pleasure of his goodness* [agathosune], *and the work of faith with power.* God wants us to have that *agathosune* kind of goodness so we may apply it in our lives as regenerated people, the recipients of God's goodness!

But there's still another Greek word for goodness—*chrestotes.* When this word is used to describe God's goodness, it denotes two aspects: (a) that which is upright and righteous, and (b) that which is good in the sense of kindness of heart or action.

Let's look at part (a) first. I'll use Romans 3:12 as an illustration: *They are all gone out of the way, they are together become unprofitable: there is none that doeth good* [chrestotes], *no, not one.* Again, God is saying there are no upright, or righteous, people. No one is righteous in himself. Therefore, if anyone is to be considered good, he must have that goodness bestowed on him by God.

Part (b) of the definition of *chrestotes* has to do with kindness of heart or action. Sometimes when the Bible uses the word *kindness*, that word could actually be translated "goodness." Romans 2:4 says, *Despisest thou the riches of his goodness and forbearance and longsuffering; not knowing that the goodness of God leadeth thee to repentance?* Again we see that God is rich in His goodness. We need to begin to tap into that rich goodness. We need to taste it and begin to receive it so we can get some experience with the goodness of God.

It is *chrestotes*, God's kindness of heart, that enables a person to turn from his wayward direction, repent, and serve God. Listen to what Romans 11:22 says about the *chrestotes* kind of God's goodness: *Behold therefore the goodness and severity of God: on them which fell, severity; but toward thee, goodness, if thou continue in his goodness: otherwise thou also shalt be cut off.* This scripture reveals that God has offered His goodness to us. But if we step back and reject that goodness, then we receive His severity.

What else are we to do about God's goodness? We are to imitate it! *Beloved, follow not that which is evil, but that which is good. He that doeth good is of God: but he that doeth evil hath not seen God* (3 John 1:11). The Greek word for *imitate* is *mimetes*. It means "to mimic." We are to *mimetes* God's goodness. We are to follow His example. Then we are to mimic that goodness—reproduce it in the same form. We are to *taste and see!* Then as we begin to mimic the good as God would have us do, we can become doers of the Word. God says when we do, even our enemies can't harm us.

Conditions of God's Goodness

Goodness has a condition, however! Even though God, in His goodness, saves us, we must believe it and receive it. That is our responsibility. It's how we must respond. His goodness comes IF we continue in His goodness. So there is yet another condition of His goodness: He requires that we continue in His goodness. We are to pursue His goodness!

See that none render evil for evil unto any man; but ever follow that which is good, both among yourselves, and to all men (1 Thessalonians 5:15). That's a commandment from Jesus Christ to the Church to continue in and follow after good! God has deposited that goodness in us, and we are to continue in it and follow after it. *For the eyes of the Lord are over the righteous, and his ears are open unto their prayers: but the face of the Lord is against them that do evil. And who is he that will harm you, if ye be followers of that which is good?* (1 Peter 3:12,13.) In this passage, the word *followers* means "to be zealous." Therefore, God is saying that He wants us to be zealous of His goodness.

But sanctify the Lord God in your hearts: and be ready always to give an answer to every man that asketh you a reason of the hope that is in you with meekness and fear: Having a good conscience; that, whereas they speak evil of you, as of evildoers, they may be ashamed that falsely accuse your good conversation in Christ (1 Peter 3:15,16).

To be zealous means "to show zeal, to be intensely enthusiastic." Sometimes we miss that. We're not really as intent as we should be about the things God has shared with us. When we are intensely enthusiastic, it works for our benefit, as revealed by the scriptures we have just examined.

Another word we might use to describe that zeal is *fervor*. When we are zealous of the things of God, we are also fervent. For some reason, we Christians have lost that fervor. Modern-day Christianity is so refined and laid back that most of us have become "laid-back Christians." We don't make too much noise or too many movements. But

God wants us to show intense enthusiasm as we continue in His *chrestotes* goodness!

As we continue in that *chrestotes,* God expects us to also express His *agathosune.* In other words, He wants that *chrestotes* we are continuing in to be expressed outwardly as His *agathosune*—moral goodness. Then in our first step toward the continuation of that *chrestotes,* we are to PROVE His goodness. Yes, there is a scripture that tells us to do that! *I beseech you therefore, brethren, by the mercies of God, that ye present your bodies a living sacrifice, holy, acceptable unto God, which is your reasonable service. And be not conformed to this world: but be ye transformed by the renewing of your mind, that ye may PROVE what is that good, and acceptable, and perfect, will of God* (Romans 12:1,2; emphasis mine).

PROVE HIS GOODNESS! Moreover, He tells us in this wonderful passage of text that it is our *responsibility* to prove His goodness! *Be not conformed to this world* [that is a command]: *but be ye transformed by the renewing of your mind, that ye may PROVE what is that good, and acceptable, and perfect, will of God.* (Emphasis mine.) We must prove that goodness! God is saying, "I want you to test Me and see how good I am!"

So the first thing we are to do as we continue in this *chrestotes* is to PROVE it. Next, we are to "cling to it." Romans 12:9 says, *Let love be without dissimulation. Abhor that which is evil; cleave* [cling] *to that which is good.* To cling to that *chrestotes* means you are to continue in it until you are stuck to it. You become joined together with it!

Ephesians 2:7 reveals something more about this *chrestotes: That in the ages to come he might shew the exceeding riches of his grace in his kindness toward us through Christ Jesus.* While the Bible translates it as *kindness*, the word used in this passage is *chrestotes*.

Once you PROVE it, then CLING to it, there's a third thing you must do with the *chrestotes* goodness of God: You must DO it! But you must not just do it—you must work it! Work at putting that *chrestotes* goodness that is filled with kindness into operation in your life! Give it all you've got!

So God offers us His goodness and requires us to continue in it, pursue it, prove it, cling to it, and do it. He's rich in it. He has enough for everyone. We can use it all the time. He wants to fill us with that goodness and put us on display. If we will just stand up, the whole universe and even the stars will clap and sing! All creation will shout, "Boy, God is good!"

But the best thing about this goodness is that it belongs to the saints! The angels cannot experience this type of goodness. That shows you how good God is right there. The angels do not have the ability to repent. Only man has been given that opportunity.

Chrestotes signifies not merely the quality of goodness, but goodness in action. Jesus is the epitome of that goodness in action. He had compassion on the poor. He had compassion on the sick. Everything He did was an illustration of His goodness in action—goodness expressing itself in deeds. Ultimately, He gave His life out of His compassion for fallen man.

Do you see why sometimes we just need to sit down and say, "Thank You, God, for Your goodness?"

Hebraic Concepts of "Good"

Now let's look at a Hebrew word for good—*hesed*. It means "love." But it means more than love. The word

The Goodness of God

hesed contains tenderness, kindness, compassion. That *hesed* love contains deeds and actions that will benefit us in every area of life. God is that *hesed* love!

John 3:16 is the essence of that *hesed* love: *For God so loved the world, that he gave his only begotten Son, that whosoever believeth in him should not perish, but have everlasting life.* (Emphasis mine.) What kindness! What mercy! What grace! In this scripture, God is showing His pity, His tenderness, His goodness, and so much more! And do you notice that in John 3:16, there is no mention of the severity of God's goodness? The severity comes in rejecting that love. How tragic that severity is! It brings fear, because when you reject that love, you become one of those who fall.

Now, there is another Hebrew word for good—*tov*. The word, *tob* or *tov* is really the main Hebrew word for "good." This word in its various forms is used to mean "that which is good to the senses, something that is agreeable." When *tov* is used, God is saying, "I want to be agreeable to you...pleasant...desirable." It also means "beautiful," as well as "that which is useful, fit, and suitable." That's why we need Him to direct our lives—so things will go well!

So the Hebrew language reveals that not only does God offer this *hesed* type of love, or goodness, but he also offers *tov*—the aspect of being good and causing things to go well.

What else does *tov* mean? It means God wants to please you! God is saying, "I'll cause things to go well because I want to please you!" Can you see how good God is? He's so good that it's mind-boggling! It's staggering!

The rich young ruler really missed it because he thought he was going to come out on the losing end when

Jesus challenged him to sell all he had. God would have caused everything to go well for him. He would have said, "I'll please you!" God would have given him back even more than he had! But Jesus understood how hard it is for those who have riches to enter into the kingdom of heaven, because they think the only good is what they can buy.

There is another meaning for *tov*—"that which is morally good, honest, being of virtue, and of being virtuous." It also means "of that which is right." And it means "fair." It was the word used to describe Sarah and some of the other maids in the Bible. So perhaps God is saying, "When you learn how to put My goodness into your life, I'll keep you looking fair!"

Tov also means "to be happy and joyful." It means "to give an advantage." It means "pleasure." When God has given you His *tov,* you don't need to seek the pleasures of sin for a season! He has made His *tov* goodness available to you, and it is beautiful, pleasurable, desirable, and of an advantage! *Taste and see* the goodness of God, and you can have all of these pleasures all of the time!

Tov is also applied to something fitting. Sometimes we get out of shape and ask God for things He knows would not be fitting to us. But, in His goodness, He holds those things back because He knows they would not be fitting. We may not like it, but that's the reality. God withholds those things that are not fitting and gives us those things that should be present in our lives.

Tov also means "that which is not only good, but true." When Jesus said, *I am...the truth* (John 14:6), He was also revealing His goodness to mankind. So, then, truth is good, and good is truth. The *tov* kind of goodness is also valuable. When you have that kind of goodness, there is no need to compare yourself to anyone else. God is saying,

"The goodness I give to you is valuable! In fact, you might not even realize how valuable it is!"

Tov can also mean "convenient." Sometimes you may get things that are not convenient. They are out of season. You say, "I should have had this two weeks ago, but here it comes now!" *Tov*—God's goodness—is always convenient. It is never late...and never early! It is always on time! It's convenient!

Another meaning for *tov* is "favorable." God is saying, "I will give you favor." *Jesus increased in wisdom and stature, and in favour with God and man* (Luke 2:52). He will also cause men to give you favor. You need that favor.

Tov is comfortable, wholesome, and contains the concept of "wholeness." It also means "kind."

But hang on to your seat for this definition: *Tov* can also mean "liberal!" That means when God gives, He's not stingy! He's lavish! He's no miser. He's no penny-pincher! He's liberal! He's good! And He doesn't get mad when He starts pouring out goodness. *If any of you lack wisdom, let him ask of God, that giveth to all men liberally, and upbraideth not; and it shall be given him* (James 1:5). And in God's goodness toward men, wisdom is just one of the things He gives. He gives abundantly. He gives above and beyond measure. *Now unto him that is able to do exceeding abundantly above all that we ask or think, according to the power that worketh in us, Unto him be glory in the church by Christ Jesus throughout all ages, world without end* (Ephesians 3:20,21). He gives even above and beyond what we ask for. Why? Because He's liberal in His *tov* goodness! He gives above measure. That's why we shouldn't be afraid to ask.

Tov also means "bountiful, beneficent, propitious, and in good condition." When God gives something, He doesn't give that which is broken-down, hand-me-down, or from the junk yard! Sometimes we may think God wants us to accept any old thing. But in reality, what God wants to give us is in good condition! So if what you have is not in good condition, you know God didn't give it to you! The deceiver tricked you. Satan offered you something, and you went for it! *Tov* means "in good condition." It also means "that which is best." God will give you the best.

The following Hebrew definitions are found on page 197 of William Wilson's *Old Testament Word Studies Lexicon and Concordance*.

The definition of the Hebrew word, *halam,* will surprise you. It might even mess up your prayer life! It means "to be made strong." God says, "When I give you My *halam* goodness, I make you strong!" Do you see how Paul picked up on that concept when he wrote, *Be strong in the Lord, and in the power of his might* (Ephesians 6:10)? Paul was a Hebrew! He understood the *halam* kind of God's goodness. He understood that God was saying, "I want to give you some goodness, and My goodness to you will make you strong." That's why Christians have the power to overcome evil with good—because possessing God's *halam* goodness is to be made strong!

The Hebrew word, *yaal,* is a verb meaning "to be useful, or to profit." Here God is saying that when He shares His goodness with us, He wants us to be useful and bring some profit forth from it. That's why He wants us to take it to the exchequer—the bank—and draw interest on what He has given to us. What happened to the man who refused to use his talent? He buried it, and it was ultimately taken from him and given to the one who had invested most wisely. (See Matthew 25:24-28.) That is the concept of *yaal.*

God wants us to be useful and profit from the good He has deposited in us.

Yashar means "to be right." It also means "that which seems good." In this word, God is saying it is good to be in His presence. "Every time you're around Me, it will just appear to you to be good!" And you will be able to respond, "It's so good, God—I just want to stay here all the time! It's that good!"

Kishron means "success." Here God is saying, *"Taste and see*—I'll make you successful!" And if God makes you successful, you'd better believe that no one can make you fall! It means "gain." It means "advantage."

Meod means that when God does something, He does it "exceedingly great." Just think about that when you pray! God always desires to exceed that which you can conceive of. He takes up where you left off. Sometimes your language will fail you when you are praying. You can't hang in there long enough. Your language will fail you and your body will get tired. But you know you need to hang in there a little more. When God gives you His *meod* goodness, He'll just take it a little bit further for you, even though you have stopped praying.

That word, *meod,* means He will also do it for you greatly! He'll go beyond. He'll multiply your efforts!

I like the word, *zaleha,* too. It means "to go on." It means, "Don't let anything stop you!" Have you ever had to go somewhere and it seemed you just couldn't make it? So you start praying. Here's a good example: A brother in our congregation is a marathon runner. A marathon is a race of 26.2 miles. When he first started running, he could get to twenty-three miles, and then his body would begin to shut down. He knew he couldn't go on, so he started praying in tongues! He started talking to the Lord, and before

How Good Is God?

he knew it, he was at the finish line! He had experienced the *zaleha* goodness of God! He was able to go on.

Zaleha also contains the concept of prosperity. My father knew all about this *zaleha*. If you wanted to make him mad, all you had to do was tell him, "I can't!" He always told me, "Never say can't, and don't ever give up!" That's *zaleha!*

The Hebrew word, *qum* (koom), means "to stand up." It also means "to cause to stand." When you have received God's *kum* goodness, you can stand!

Shalam means "I will restore." How wonderful! This quality of God's goodness means that He is able to restore. And that means that you and I have never lost anything— because God will restore that which has been lost! He is saying, in *shalam,* "I'll restore it! I'll restore it! I'll restore it!"

Shalam also means "to requite or pay back." So not only will God restore to you that which is lost, but He will also pay back your enemies. *Taste and see that the Lord is good*, and you won't have vengeance in mind. You'll be able to rest in God as He takes care of everything. It also means "to recompense." That is God saying, "I'll make it good! Whatever you come to Me with, I'll make it good!"

Finally there is the Hebrew word, *shaphar,* which means "acceptable." When you receive His *shaphar* goodness, He has made you acceptable to Himself. You are *accepted in the beloved* (Ephesians 1:6). You will be able to say with confidence, "I am accepted!" Everyone else might reject you...everyone else might forsake you...everyone else might walk away and leave you behind, but God says, *I will never leave thee, nor forsake thee* (Hebrews 13:5). Why? Because you're acceptable! *"O taste and see* that I have given you some *shaphar!"*

The Godhead Is Good!

God is the author of all that is good. And by being the author of all that is good, He is also the cause and effect of all that is good. Normally this goodness comes through the person of Jesus Christ. Jesus is the chief vessel of God's goodness unto us. But let's expand this a little further.

God is a triune being. And God is good. Even though most of that goodness is expressed to us through the person of Jesus Christ, all of the divine offices of the Godhead—Father, Son, and Holy Spirit—are good. If we are to understand the goodness of God and really see how good God is, then we must separate out the purposes of the Godhead for our own teaching purposes. Then we will be able to see how God ministers His goodness to us through Himself, the Father; through Jesus, the Son; and through the Holy Spirit.

In Romans 1:20, Paul wrote, *For the invisible things of him from the creation of the world are clearly seen, being understood by the things that are made, even his eternal power and Godhead; so that they are without excuse.* So all three offices of the Godhead are eternal. God is backing His Word and His goodness with all the power of the eternal Godhead, that we might be without excuse. In other words, if we are not experiencing the goodness of God, whose fault is it? Is it God's fault? Has He withheld any of that goodness from us? Is He unequal? Is He unjust? No! It is our failure to receive! We are without excuse!

The Father Is Good

We must remember that God has only good designs toward His people. Learn that! Not only is God good, but He has only good designs toward His people! He wants the best for you and me! Notice how God handled David. He never rubbed in his face the situation with Bathsheba. He has never rubbed a former sin into the face of anyone. He won't do it to you and me, either! God is good, and He wants the best for us. We have often falsely accused God and wondered, "Why is God doing this?"

Perhaps God is not doing it! Your problem, then, IS NOT WITH GOD! He has provided good things for you, and He is faithful to perform all His promises. Every one of His promises are good and true. He doesn't make bad promises! Why? Because God is good! He is the cause and the effect of all that is good!

Sadly, however, Americans have not taught their children correctly concerning this good God. Primarily for the purpose of discipline in the home, children have been taught from an early age to view God as a stern, authoritarian figure who is constantly observing them, watchful to punish every wrong deed. Many American parents have told their children, "You'd better be good, or GOD WILL GET YOU!"

Some claim to be Christian parents, yet they present a picture to their child that portrays God as a monster! Then they wonder why that child, when he becomes a teenager, wants nothing more than to get as far away from this avenging God as possible. When he hears something like *"You'd better be good, or GOD WILL GET YOU!"* over and over again throughout his early years, he'll eventually get to the point that he will no longer respond to it. But that concept of a vengeful God is still in there—it's instilled in him. And sooner or later, that wrong concept of God is going to pop up.

In other words, many of us have had ingrained in us the idea that we must be good at all times or God will not respond to us! But if we teach that God is good, then we must also teach about His grace and mercy.

For according to His grace, His goodness is shown to us. It is not limited to anybody! His mercy, however, is NOT shown to everybody! His goodness, He says, *I will show to all generations.* He's GOOD to everybody, but merciful to those who call upon Him. Hebrews 4:16 tells us, *Let us therefore come boldly unto the throne of grace, that we may obtain mercy, and find grace to help in time of need.* When we know of God's goodness, we can boldly obtain His mercy!

His mercy comes when we KNOW Him! The problem is that a lot of us don't know God. We're guessing...we're speculating...and we're hoping. We're designing...and sometimes we even make Him what we want Him to be. But we don't KNOW Him! God, however, is the Creator, which means we can't create anything apart from Him. And we certainly cannot create Him! He's already set! And He tells us in His Word that He's not going to change.

God, the Father, is good, and He designs good things for us. His promises are good, and He bestows on us all of His goodness, if only we will *taste and see.*

The Son Is Good

You have already seen that the Father is good. Now let's see how good the Son is, because this goodness in the Son is the goodness that is most often expressed to mankind. Watch what Colossians 2:9 says about the goodness of the Son: *For in him dwelleth all the fulness of the Godhead bodily.* So if the Father is good and if all of the Godhead's fulness also dwells in the Son, then all of the Father's goodness is also present in the Son! And that's good!

The word *fullness* in the Greek is defined as "full, fulness," and I like that! What it really means, then, is "full to running over." It's what the psalmist meant when he wrote, *My cup runneth over* (Psalm 23:5). It is God saying, "I will fill it up, and then I will go beyond the fill." Jesus represents *all the fulness of the Godhead bodily,* meaning that in His human existence here on earth, He never once lost the goodness of God. In fact, we see Him constantly going *about doing good, and healing all that were* [sick and] *oppressed of the devil* (Acts 10:38). What was He doing? He was expressing the fullness of the nature of God, the Father—which is GOOD!

People came from miles and miles around to receive that goodness. All we must do is go back and look at the life of Jesus to see just how good He really was. He was too good! In my daily reading of the Word, I recently came across the story of the grieving widow who had lost her only son. The funeral procession was in progress as Jesus passed by. The eldest son was important in ancient Jewish society because he was the one assigned to care for his aging parents. To have no living son meant that this woman's care in her old age might not be provided. If you didn't have a son to provide for you in those days, you were lost!

Jesus saw the procession and all the mourners. When He inquired about it, He was told that it was a funeral for the son of a widow. Jesus immediately wanted to do good. He did something that He normally did not do in that day. He stretched out His hand, put it on the bier, and raised the woman's son from the dead.

Now, it's a good thing to be raised from the dead. But this story is about more than being raised from the dead. This raising of the son meant a restoration of the widow's provision for her old age. Now she knew she would not be forced to become a beggar on the street one day.

The Goodness of God

Jesus is the Good Shepherd who laid down His life for the sheep, and that's a good place to start in describing how good God is! How many people do you know who would die for you? Some will kill for you, but not many will die—not even for a righteous man. Jesus died for sinners. In fact, it was His destiny to lay down His life for the sheep.

He is the fountain of all grace and goodness to the Church. And He administers that goodness to His Body, the believers. Just think about that! He's a fountain of goodness! That means if you go to drink from that fountain, you will never be able to consume it all! You will never be able to dry up that fountain of life, which is God's goodness to His Church. Don't worry if others drink from it too! They can never drink it all! There's no need to become angry because someone else is receiving God's blessing above and beyond what they have asked! Your turn is coming! Just drink!

Just be concerned with what God has promised to you, and don't be concerned with what He's doing for someone else. If you understand that this fountain will never run dry, you will realize there's enough goodness there for everyone. In fact, everyone in the world can receive this goodness, and God will still have an abundant supply in reserve! There will always be plenty for you!

You see, God's resources are not limited. The resources of earth are limited, but His resources are endless. Even limited by His bodily form, Jesus was able to do good to those of His day. How much more is He able to express that goodness to us today, now that He has ascended on high!

The Son is good! He has wrought a good work for all who believe in redemption. Let's just think about that.

We're REDEEMED! That's the greatest work we could ever think of! He's our Redeemer.

He's also our Advocate (1 John 2:1). Right now the Son is in heaven, standing up for us in the court of God. When we blow it, He's right there, taking our part as our Advocate. He says, "Judge, can I speak for a moment on behalf of this little one who doesn't really know what he's doing? I want to be an advocate for this little sheep with the big head that doesn't have too much in it! That's the problem, Judge. He's dealing with his head instead of his heart!"

So the Judge says, "Will You stand in his behalf?" And the Son says, "I'll stand for him! He belongs to Me. I'm his Shepherd." Then, when you ask Jesus, the Son, "How much is all this going to cost me?" He just smiles and says, "It's free!" Oh, man! It truly is the goodness of God that brings us to repentence! (Romans 2:4.)

Now I'm not saying you won't reap what you sow (Galatians 6:7,8), but when Jesus is in your corner, and you repent of any wrongdoing, He can help you kill a bad crop! And simply because you believed, you get all this grace! All this goodness! Just think about that! That's how good the Son is!

The Holy Spirit Is Good

We have already learned that Jesus represented *all the fulness of the Godhead bodily* (Colossians 2:9), but Jesus had to go away. Before He departed earth, He said, "I'm going to leave you some more goodness! You can't get away from My goodness!" And He sent the Holy Spirit. Jesus said it was "expedient" for us that He went away. Why? Because the Holy Spirit is good, too, and He would dwell with us twenty-four hours a day.

The Father is good. He passed that goodness down to us through His Son. And the Son went away, but not before passing that same goodness along to us through the Holy Spirit. Let's look at John 16:13,14: *Howbeit when he, the Spirit of truth, is come, he will guide you into all truth: for he shall not speak of himself; but whatsoever he shall hear, that shall he speak: and he will shew you things to come. He shall glorify me: for he shall receive of mine, and shall shew it unto you.*

Do you see that no matter how you deal with the Godhead, the result is good?

The Holy Spirit works good things in our hearts. Notice these verses in John, chapter 16. The Holy Spirit takes the things of the Son, enters your heart, and begins helping you to put those qualities into operation in earthly manifestation in your daily life. So not only does God pour out His goodness on you, but He helps you to express it outwardly and to live in the fullness of all that goodness.

It's hard to demonstrate that goodness without the Helper present. Remember when you were a kid and your mama told you not to touch some particular thing? "Don't touch!" But you just had to examine it. Curiosity led you right over to it, where you picked it up...dropped it...and it broke into a million pieces! "Oh, no! I just wanted to feel it!" Remember how hard it was to resist doing something you weren't supposed to do before the Helper, the Holy Spirit, entered your life to help you demonstrate goodness?

Through the Holy Spirit, God is saying, "My goodness can be manifested. O taste and you can see it now, because I have made the Holy Spirit available to you, and He will manifest My goodness in your heart! He will take of the Father, and of the Son, and reveal those things to you!"

What else does the Holy Spirit do? He shows good things to us. He doesn't want us walking around in darkness. He wants to show us what is good, what is right, what is true. *O taste and see...*and you will find out, or discern, how good God is, through the presence of the Holy Spirit. For once we taste, we will be able to discern. Let's look at Psalm 119:103: *How sweet are thy words unto my taste! yea, sweeter than honey to my mouth!* Now you are discerning how good God really is! And that's sweet—sweeter than honey! You have made a comparison and are thus able to discern. But only those who have been regenerated are able to taste that sweetness.

How good is God? He's real good! He is so good, in fact, that it takes three Greek words and eleven Hebrew words to describe how good He is! Then it takes a bunch of English words—words like absolutely, infinitely, inherently, and ineffably—to even begin to describe how good God is!

Chapter 5

Trusting in God's Goodness

We need to learn to trust in the goodness of God. Things are changing so rapidly in today's world that it is dangerous to place our confidence in governments, systems, or anything else except the Word of God. We must not look to "Egypt" for our supply, as Israel once did, or to any other nations, situations, or circumstances. God wants us to look only to Him! He wants us to trust in Him. After all, He is an abundant God. When He does anything, He does it real big! He does it on a grand scale. He goes beyond what is required when we look to Him as the Source of our supply. He is more than enough! He is able to do *exceeding abundantly above all that we ask or think* (Ephesians 3:20).

Today's truth is that God's Word is the ONLY trustworthy and reliable source. This truth is something we must all make a reality in our lives. We must learn to say with the psalmist, *O taste and see that the Lord is good: blessed is the man that trusteth in him* (Psalm 34:8).

Every taste we take of the Word of God should increase our sense of trust in the Lord! It should be easy to trust in God, once we *taste and see* how good He is! Yet I hear it all the time: "I'm having a hard time trusting God!" Maybe you aren't tasting of His goodness! Maybe you just gave it a little superficial taste! Or maybe you don't even know what you're tasting. Perhaps your sense of taste hasn't changed from the way it was when you were still living in sin.

The person who has a problem trusting is probably also having a problem tasting! In Psalm 34:8, the psalmist says that once you taste, something is going to happen. A revelation of God's goodness will stimulate within you the ability to trust in Him! Throughout the Bible, there are scriptures concerning the blessings of trusting the Lord. There are blessings that come to the man or woman who is able to trust in the Lord.

To Trust God Is to be Blessed

Let's look at Psalm 2:12, *Kiss the Son, lest he be angry, and ye perish from the way, when his wrath is kindled but a little. Blessed are all they that put their trust in him.*

A *targum* is an ancient paraphrase of the Hebrew scriptures. I like what the *targum* of Psalm 2:12 says: "Blessed are they that put their trust in His Word." Oh, I like that! Because now, not only do I have a Person to trust in, but I have the reality of His Word, and I can look at it and receive it right now! The *targum* implies that God and His Word are One—inseparable!

Remember what the *targum* says: We are blessed when we trust in God's Word. Let's look at Luke 5:5-9 for more proof that the *targum* is true: *And Simon answering said unto him, Master, we have toiled all the night, and have taken nothing: nevertheless AT THY WORD I will let down the net. And when they had this done, they inclosed a great multitude of fishes: and their net brake. And they beckoned unto their partners, which were in the other ship, that they should come and help them. And they came, and filled both the ships, so that they began to sink. When Simon Peter saw it, he fell down at Jesus' knees, saying, Depart from me; for I am a sinful man, O Lord. For he was astonished, and all that were with him, at the draught of the fishes which they had taken.* (Emphasis mine.)

Here was Simon Peter, fishing all night long with no success. He had not caught even a single fish. Suddenly Jesus tells him to cast his net *out into the deep* (v. 4). Simon might have reasoned that his toil had already produced no results, so why bother? But he trusted in Jesus' Word. *Nevertheless at thy word I will let down the net* (v. 5), Simon replied. He was blessed when he finally said, "Let's trust! Let's do it the way God said to do it, even though we've been doing this all night!" He saw immediate results of God's goodness, based upon his trust.

I like using the example of Peter because he was a man like you and me. He was stubborn. Sometimes Peter was found doing what he was supposed to do, and sometimes he wasn't. That's you and me in the mirror.

Now, watch how good God is! *And when they had this done, they inclosed a great multitude of fishes: and their net brake* (v. 6). Hey, a multitude of fishes is a whole lot of fish! This was a great multitude! There were so many fish, Peter's net broke. So he beckoned to his partners. Have you noticed? You'll have a lot of partners when God is blessing you! All of a sudden you'll find a lot of people who want to be your friend. Peter's partners came from the other ships and helped him. They just kept hauling in more fish! They netted so many fish that, according to verse 7, both ships became filled and *began to sink*!

Because Peter said, "I'm going to trust in His Word," they all became blessed and saw how good God is. When Simon Peter saw what had just happened, *he fell down at Jesus' knees, saying, Depart from me; for I am a sinful man,*

O Lord (v. 8). Why did he say that? He had just been blessed!

God's Abundant Blessings

Isaiah 6:5 may shed some light on Peter's reaction to being so blessed: *Then said I, Woe is me! for I am undone; because I am a man of unclean lips, and I dwell in the midst of a people of unclean lips: for mine eyes have seen the King, the Lord of hosts.*

Now that word *undone* means, "I am just so excited that I feel like I'm going to come apart!" Have you ever been that way? Have you ever seen little kids when they are that excited? They just don't know what to do! They don't know whether to stand up, sit down, or play. And if they decide to play, they don't know which toy to play with. They just act like they're about to come apart!

That's how Isaiah was reacting. Why? Isaiah was saying, "Man, do I really deserve all this? I know what is within me, and based on that, it's just not possible! Hey, I'm a man of unclean lips, and I dwell in the midst of a people of unclean lips. Yet I have seen the King, the Lord of hosts!"

Peter was a little like that after seeing the great multitude of fishes that were hauled in simply because he had obeyed the Lord's Word. "Hey, I'm falling apart right now because I know I am a sinful man, and I just don't deserve this! I've been a fisherman all of my life, but I've never seen anything like this! I know what fish are, and I know how to catch them, but I've never had a catch like this!" He just fell apart.

Luke 5:9 says, *For he was astonished.* In other words, Peter was saying, "I'm just so excited, I don't know what to do!" Not only was Peter astonished, but so were the men who were with him: *James, and John, the sons of Zebedee, which were partners with Simon. And Jesus said unto Simon, Fear not; from henceforth thou shalt catch men* (v. 10). Jesus was saying, "Be of courage! Don't fall apart! These things happen around Me all the time! So don't lose your cool!"

He was saying, "Hey, don't get so upset and excited! Be of courage! As long as you are tasting of Me and discerning the things of Me and putting your trust in My Word, I am able to do good! You just proved what the psalmist said—that I am good to you! I was just showing you how good I can be, and I showed your friends, too! You went out there with one net and I sent so many fish your way that one net couldn't hold them all. Even one ship couldn't hold them all! You would have settled for one net full! But I'm good! Now you have seen the abundance of the goodness of God!"

How good is God? He's so good that He was able to take that which was nothing and make it something that went far beyond simply satisfying what Simon Peter would have settled for. He said, "You'd better call your partners because the catch I've got for you, that one little net and that one ship can't handle! I'm not going to just give you enough to fill one little old net so you can go and sell a few fish and make a little bit of money! I'm going to give you enough to share!"

The result was a miracle that undoubtedly became the talk of the fish market. "Hey, what did you guys do?" What did Jesus tell Simon? *Fear not; from henceforth thou shalt catch men* (v. 10). Believe me, when you start telling others how good God is, you'll catch them, too! Because everybody wants something good.

Finally verse 11 tells us what resulted in the lives of the men who participated in that miraculous haul: *And when they had brought their ships to land, they forsook all, and followed him.* Suddenly they understood! "Boy, we can really follow God! We won't lose anything! We can forget fishing! We can go out there now and become fishers of men, and not lose anything!"

On the spot, they gave up their business, forsook all, and followed Jesus, because they realized that it was more beneficial to follow Him than to be out on their own. On their own, they might have caught a few fish in their little old nets. But Jesus was saying, "You've got to have more than one net—and boats too—in order to get all that I've got for you!"

Worthy of Praise

So we see that trusting in God's Word is also trusting in Him. Now let's look at Psalm 100:5: *For the Lord is good; his mercy is everlasting; and his truth endureth to all generations.* Here we find that not only is the Lord good, but His truth endures to all generations!

Again Psalm 135:3 underscores God's goodness. *Praise the Lord; for the Lord is good: sing praises unto his name; for it is pleasant.* Now that we know God is good, what must we do? Praise Him! We ought to praise the Lord for His goodness! Verse 5 says, *For I know that the Lord is great, and that our Lord is above all gods.* Not only is He GOOD, He is GREAT! *Whatsoever the Lord pleased, that did he in heaven, and in earth, in the seas, and all deep places* (v. 6). When you pray the disciple's prayer, "Thy kingdom come; Thy will be done in heaven, as it is on earth," you are acknowledging what Psalm 135:6 says. You are saying, "Father, I'm going to give You room to do what

You did in heaven, so it can also be done here on earth." God will do as He pleases, and He pleases to do GOOD!

David learned to trust God. Instead of going to a priest to make a sacrifice on his behalf, David went directly to God. He appealed to His nature, and in the process discovered His goodness. Then David wrote the Psalms to glorify God and to tell us something about what he had discovered. David was telling us, "You don't have to slip as far as I slipped! All you need to do in life is taste the things of God on a consistent basis. Then you'll find out about God. You'll get some experience. You'll learn to trust Him. And the more you taste, the more you'll trust...and the more you trust, the more you'll taste! It will just become a reciprocal experience!"

God Wants To Deal Bountifully

I have discovered that the goodness of God is the essential perfection of the divine nature that inclines God to deal bountifully with His creatures. Goodness is essential to God. It is the essence of God. God is good, and because it is His nature to be good, He wants to deal bountifully with mankind.

I like that word *bountifully*. In fact, I looked it up because I wanted to see its meaning in Hebrew. The Hebrew word for *bountifully* is *gamal*. It is the same root word from which we get the word, *camel*, an animal renowned for its ability to store up food and resources for long periods of time, making it ideal for desert climates. *Gamal* means "to treat a person well." God knows how to treat you, and He will treat you well! *Gamal* means "to grant benefits to a person, and to do them good!"

Let's look at this concept of God's bountiful dealings with mankind. In Psalm 13, David writes: *I will sing unto the Lord, because he hath dealt bountifully with me* (v. 6). Psalm 13, however, begins on a note of questioning: *How long wilt thou forget me, O Lord? for ever? how long wilt thou hide thy face from me?* (v. 1). As the Psalm progresses, we realize—along with David—that it may have appeared that God forgot him, but in actuality, He did not. God will never forget! That revelation caused David to sing praise to God...*because he hath dealt bountifully with me.* David found out that God was bountiful, and he said, "God knows how to treat me well! So I'm going to sing to Him! I'm going to praise Him! He knows how to grant me benefits!"

God Will Never Forget

Have you ever felt you were forgotten by God? Sometimes it may appear so. But once you understand His essential nature, as David did, you will soon realize that God will never forsake or forget His people. His goodness just will not allow Him to forget. Remember, His Word says, *I will never leave thee, nor forsake thee* (Hebrews 13:5). Even if He could, He wouldn't! That promise is God saying to us, "You might forget Me, and you might even try to forsake Me, but I'll run you down! And when you finally look up, you'll see that I caught you, and you'll finally get up and get on with what you are supposed to be doing!"

Psalm 116 is another Psalm in which David complains to God: *The sorrows of death compassed me, and the pains of hell gat hold upon me: I found trouble and sorrow* (v. 3). David was afraid! But when he finally got a hold of himself, he realized that God had been with him all along. He was probably feeling shame-faced! Have you ever felt that way? You've been complaining to God and all of a sudden you realize that things were working for your good all along! Then you say, like David did, "Ah, God, I didn't mean that! I was joking!" Then God says, "No, you weren't joking, but it's all right!" *Return unto thy rest, O my soul; for the Lord hath dealt bountifully with thee* (v. 7).

God is saying, "Rest in Me! Rest in the fact that you know you have tasted and discovered some things about Me! Rest in that! Rest!" Rest, you see, is a picture of absolute trust!

Why was David able to rest and trust God? Because of what he realized next: *For thou hast delivered my soul from death, mine eyes from tears, and my feet from falling. I will walk before the Lord in the land of the living. I believed, therefore have I spoken: I was greatly afflicted: I said in my haste, All men are liars. What shall I render unto the Lord for all his benefits toward me? I will take the cup of salvation, and call upon the name of the Lord* (Psalm 116:8-13).

We see that, by now, David is speaking from his own experience. But he is also speaking from the revelation that God is good! In the midst of great affliction, David discovered something. *What shall I render unto the Lord for all his benefits toward me?* (v. 12). David then realized there was nothing he could do except take the cup of salvation and call upon the name of the Lord! That's all he could do! That's all any of us can do!

Psalm 119 is also rich in its portrayal of the bountiful goodness of God. Psalm 119, the longest of the Psalms, is broken up into twenty-two sections that correspond with the Hebrew alphabet. Since we are discussing God's bountiful, or *gamal*, dealings with His people, we will look at the section called *Gimel,* which begins at verse 17. It is actually the same root as *gamal* and, as I stated earlier, the same root as *camel.* We can learn something from the camel! When the camel bows down, the Master loads him up! *Deal bountifully with thy servant, that I may live, and keep thy word* (Psalm 119:17).

In this verse, the psalmist is saying, "Lord, in keeping Your Word, I am being drawn into more and more trust. And since I trust You, I'll have more and more bounty and I'll be living real good! Be bountiful to Your servant, Lord! Just be what You are by Your nature!"

That's good! Now we'll make the application of what David was talking about. *But this I say, He which soweth sparingly shall reap also sparingly; and he which soweth bountifully shall reap also bountifully* (2 Corinthians 9:6). Paul is saying that if we sow bountifully—like God does—we will also reap bountifully. All God is asking us to do is take a little from what He has given and give it back to Him. He is saying, "You be bountiful with Me, and I'll be bountiful with you! Just trust in My Word!"

When you do that, you can say, "Lord, just deal bountifully with me because I'm Your servant! Deal bountifully! It's part of Your nature! Do good!"

Happiness and Well-Being

God's blessing is aimed at promoting two things among His creatures: Happiness and well-being. Notice I said, "among His creatures!" God wants us to be happy! He wants us to live in prosperity. Yes, God's goodness provides our necessities, but He also supplies our conveniences.

Sometimes we try to be "super-duper" spiritual! We say, "Well, I don't need much! I don't need to have running water! I just want to serve the Lord!" That sounds real spiritual, but just go out in the jungle where there is no opportunity to take a shower for ten days.

That happened to me! I went ten days without a shower...just washing from a little bucket. I was grateful for the water, but I was not very happy about the way I was getting it!

What I'm getting at is that God's nature is so GOOD that it promotes both our happiness AND our well-being. That includes the supply of our necessities AND our conveniences.

Let me illustrate the difference between necessities and conveniences. I can't presume that every time I turn on the hot water there will be an ample supply! That hot water is not a necessity! Millions of people in the world do not have hot water. Hot water is a convenience! Yet most of us don't even take the time to thank God for this convenience.

I'd be glad to ride a donkey, if all I had was a donkey for transportation. Then a donkey would be a necessity, not a convenience. However, if a better mode of transportation—a more convenient one—was available to me, I should not presume upon God because I have more than the man who can only ride a donkey. I'm glad I don't have to ride a donkey, but I'm not putting down the man who does!

When you adjust your perspective about these things, you'll find that it will change your whole conversation with God. Suddenly you will be aware of all the good things He is allowing you to take advantage of. When you realize the many conveniences He has blessed you with, it will take you out of that "poor me" syndrome. Then you will start actually realizing the many good things you do have!

Remember, there is nothing within you or me that is deserving of these good things. It is nothing good in you or me that attracts the blessings of God. God sends these good things because He wants to be a part of our necessities and our conveniences. He wants to be involved in the natural pleasures of life.

I like the Ethiopian translation of Philippians 4:19. It changes just one word—using *will* for *shall*—but that one small word makes a big difference. *But my God WILL supply all your need according to his riches in glory by Christ Jesus.* (Emphasis mine.) The Ethiopians, in their translation, interpreted Philippians 4:19 to be a promise. I like that!

As we have already seen, all goodness in God's creation issues directly from Him. There is no good apart from the goodness that God supplies. So if we need that goodness, God said He will supply it. (See Philippians 4:19.) God is saying, "What do you need? I'll supply it! Just tell Me what you need!"

That's a promise! What will God do? He will supply ALL of our needs! Paul emphasized the word *God* in Philippians 4:19. What he was saying was, "This is not just any god. This is MY God, the God I have tasted, the God of all grace, the God of nature, and the God of providence. He WILL supply all the necessities of life, and even the natural pleasures of life! I can trust in Him!" *If God be for us, who can be against us?* (Romans 8:31.)

We use Romans 8:31 most when we are talking about spiritual warfare—and we need to be aware of spiritual warfare. But Romans 8:31 means much more than that. Sometimes we should just meditate on this verse and realize, "Since God is for me, I have the abundance of my necessities and the use of conveniences! Because God is for me, I can actually experience the natural pleasures in life!"

The key, however, is that all these blessings are ours, not because we are for God, but because God is for US! God's goodness works differently than any of His other qualities. God will be good to both the righteous and the unrighteous. Yes, that's in the Bible! God won't show His mercies to everyone. But His goodness is another matter. He shows His goodness to all.

Chapter 6

God Is Good to All

We have already seen that man's goodness is not resident within himself. He acquires it from God. There is no one good. We must understand this because only when we do are we able to draw what we need from God.

However, there are many things we don't want to take to God because we think we're good enough to handle them ourselves. About 90 percent of the time, we say, "I can handle it!" When we are driving our cars, for instance, we don't ask God to help us. We just get behind the wheel and drive off! But there is always a blind spot in the mirror.

I was driving recently and getting ready to make a lane change. I didn't look too closely at that blind spot, but something told me, "You'd better look again!" Suddenly there was a big brown car, right there on my tail. If I had made a move, it all would have been over. I might have thought, "I'm a good driver!" and disregarded that small warning. However, I didn't even pray about it—I just heeded that small voice, and now I can reflect on it. God spared me from an accident, but not because I was a real good driver. Good drivers die every day. It's the protected drivers who are still alive. God protected me because He's good.

We need to get this particular concept down, so God can begin to lift us up. It's only when we learn to trust God absolutely that we realize, "There's nothing good in me—nothing at all!"

But God's inclination to deal bountifully with man is not confined or limited to those who obey. It's not because we try to be good and obey God that we are blessed with His goodness. Yes, our parents told us, "You'd better be good!" They've even connected the concept to the guy in the red suit, "You'd better be good or Santa Claus won't bring you a gift!" Too often we try to apply this same concept of qualifying for God's goodness to our Christian walk.

We have the mistaken idea that God is good to us because we obey or have certain qualities of goodness present within ourselves. Therefore, we reason, God will be good to us. Not necessarily! He could be, because it's His nature to be good. But Matthew 5:45 says, *That ye may be the children of your Father which is in heaven: for he maketh his sun to rise on the evil and on the good, and sendeth rain on the just and on the unjust.* Now, rain is good, but whether you obey God or not, you'll still get wet! God is trying to show us that we must be aware of His nature so we can humble ourselves and draw from that quality of His goodness. We must see that everything we have is based upon His goodness.

Drawing From God's Goodness

How, then, do we draw upon God's goodness? First, we need to consider how good God has been to us. Then we'll find out how good God WILL be to us. We've got to put this in our remembrance. David said, *O taste and see*...then you'll find out you are blessed. When we realize that, in ourselves, we are not good but God is ALWAYS good, we have the ability to draw from that goodness. That's when we realize that God shows His goodness to

ALL because His goodness is continual. It is not limited, nor is it conditioned by the attitude of those to whom it flows.

In other words, God is not going to bless you because you have some conditional attitude! If you think God will bless you simply because you show Him how good you are, you're wrong! Just be yourself! Goodness belongs solely to God. It's not based on what you think about me or what I think about you. It's not conditional. It's based upon the nature of God.

Paul emphasized this in Romans 5:6-8: *For when we were yet without strength, in due time Christ died for the ungodly. For scarcely for a righteous man will one die: yet peradventure for a good man some would even dare to die. But God commendeth his love toward us, in that, while we were yet sinners, Christ died for us.* Did you catch that? God was good to you even when you were ungodly! He showed you how good He is even when you were not worthwhile. Now, if God did that for you in the beginning of your Christian walk, how much more will He do once you have tasted and discovered how good God really is!

You see, God deals with all men according to the principle of divine goodness. Augustine wrote: *"Good for good, evil for evil—that is natural. Evil for good—that is devilish. Good for evil—that is God."* That, I think, is a very good definition of the principle of divine goodness.

Luke 6:35 teaches us about God's impartiality in His goodness: *But love ye your enemies, and do good, and lend, hoping for nothing again; and your reward shall be great, and ye shall be the children of the Highest: for he is kind unto the unthankful and to the evil.* Here is yet another verification that God is good to all. He's good across the board to everybody. His goodness, unlike His grace or His mercy, has no limitations. He says, "I'll be merciful to whom I decide...but I'll show My goodness to all generations. I'll show My goodness to the just, the unjust, the good, the evil, the thankful, and the unthankful! I'll just be GOOD!"

So you can see, then, that God will not be "more good" to people who try to be good, or "less good" to those who are evil.

Aren't you glad that God's goodness is not based upon your being good? Remember when your mother said, "You be good and I'll give you a cookie?" You still weren't good, but she overlooked the way you were acting up and gave you the cookie anyway! That's what this great, bountiful quality of God's goodness is like.

God Reveals His Goodness

Early in God's revelation of Himself to His people, God began to instruct them concerning His goodness. *The Lord descended in the cloud, and stood with him* [Moses] *there, and proclaimed the name of the Lord. And the Lord passed by before him, and proclaimed, The Lord, The Lord God, merciful and gracious, longsuffering, and abundant in goodness and truth, Keeping mercy for thousands, forgiving iniquity and transgression and sin, and that will by no means clear the guilty; visiting the iniquity of the fathers upon the children, and upon the children's children, unto the third and to the fourth generation* (Exodus 34:5-7).

In his encounter with Jehovah, Moses learned six things about the Lord:

- He is merciful.
- He is gracious.
- He is longsuffering.

- He is abundant in goodness.
- He is true.
- He will by no means clear the guilty.

Because of His goodness, God isn't going to let you off! You're going to have to deal with the issue of sin, and even the issue of the sins of the fathers. What He is saying is this: "If you continue to follow in the ways of your parents—if you sin against Me like they did—then the same things will happen to you that happened to them. And if you teach your children the same sins by not getting them out of your own life, the same things will happen to your children that happened to you!"

The key words in this passage of Exodus, however, are still *merciful, gracious, longsuffering, and abundant in goodness* and in *truth.* God doesn't want you to be guilty! God was not standing over Israel ready to beat them if they don't fall into line. He was opening His arms to them and offering them salvation and DELIVERANCE from their sins and the sins of their fathers.

Let's look at what Isaiah said many years later: *I will mention the lovingkindnesses of the Lord, and the praises of the Lord, according to all that the Lord hath bestowed on us, and the great goodness toward the house of Israel, which he hath bestowed on them according to his mercies, and according to the multitude of his lovingkindnesses* (Isaiah 63:7).

Do you mention the Lord's lovingkindnesses? You should mention them to others and even to yourself. Have you ever said, "Father, I just want to mention Your lovingkindnesses. Your Word says Your lovingkindness is better than life?" (Psalm 63:3.) That scripture is saying that it's better to know about the lovingkindness of the Lord than it is to live, because you can't live without His lovingkindness. Unless you know about His lovingkindess, you're going to have a very miserable life.

But I know that if God was good to Israel, He will be good to me too. I can make an application of Isaiah 63:7. He is not only good, but He is abundantly good! He is greatly good!

Recipients of God's Goodness

Are some people recipients of more of God's goodness than others? Do some people—especially among Christians—receive more of certain things than others receive?

Most of us who know the Lord experience times when it seems there are some who are more blessed than others. If we aren't careful, Satan will use the lie that some are more blessed than others to work on our minds and emotions. Then we become envious and jealous of one another, thinking God is allowing some of us to have more and some to have less.

To understand this complex issue of why some seem to be blessed more than others, let's look at the first recorded lie of Satan. The first thing Satan did was to cast an aspersion on the goodness of God. We need to be aware of that. Satan attacked God's goodness and began to undermine it. He began to fill Eve's mind with questions—questions that caused her to wonder about God's goodness.

We need to be aware of Satan's lies so we won't be caught in a satanic attack when we see others receiving from God and it appears we are receiving less. We need to learn to think like God thinks, not like the devil thinks—at least to the degree He will allow us to learn.

In Genesis, chapter 3, we see this first recorded attack by the devil against God's goodness. We've probably read this passage many times, but perhaps not in this particular light. *Now the serpent was more subtil than any beast of the field which the Lord God had made. And he said unto the woman, Yea, hath God said, Ye shall not eat of every tree of the garden? And the woman said unto the serpent, We may eat of the fruit of the trees of the garden: But of the fruit of the tree which is in the midst of the garden, God hath said, Ye shall not eat of it, neither shall ye touch it, lest ye die. And the serpent said unto the woman, Ye shall not surely die: For God doth know that in the day ye eat thereof, then your eyes shall be opened, and ye shall be as gods, knowing good and evil. And when the woman saw that the tree was good for food, and that it was pleasant to the eyes, and a tree to be desired to make one wise, she took of the fruit thereof, and did eat, and gave also unto her husband with her; and he did eat* (Genesis 3:1-6).

Remember, God prepared all things for us to eat, and they were good. But there was one tree that was forbidden. The serpent went to work on Eve's imagination, casting an aspersion on God's goodness until she *saw that the tree was good for food.* Eve said to the devil, *We may eat of the fruit of the trees of the garden: But of the fruit of the tree which is in the midst of the garden, God hath said, Ye shall not eat of it, neither shall ye touch it, lest ye die* (vv. 2,3). Now go back and read what God said about that tree in Genesis 2:17: *But of the tree of the knowledge of good and evil, thou shalt not eat of it: for in the day that thou eatest thereof thou shalt surely die.* What Eve said to the devil was not what God originally said about the forbidden tree.

But the devil had cast an aspersion on God's goodness. He took advantage of the fact that God had provided

The Goodness of God

all the food in the garden for the man and the woman to eat. And it was good! There was just one prohibition! The woman even got the prohibition mixed up, because she called it the *tree in the midst of the garden.* God did not call it the tree in the midst of the garden. He called it *the tree of the knowledge of good and evil* (Genesis 2:17). The tree of life, not the tree of the knowledge of good and evil, was the tree that was located in the midst of the garden. (Genesis 2:9.) God definitely wants us to eat of the tree of life! How do we know this? He tells us in Revelation 22:14!

But the devil said to Eve, *Ye shall not surely die: For God doth know that in the day ye eat thereof, then your eyes shall be opened, and ye shall be as gods, knowing good and evil* (Genesis 3:4,5). Another lie! Satan told the woman that after she ate the fruit of the tree, her eyes would be opened. Yet in reality, eating the forbidden fruit caused the eyes of both the man and the woman to be closed to the things of God.

Acts 26:18 tells us that we are in the process of bringing people *to open their eyes, and to turn them from darkness to light, and from the power of Satan unto God, that they may receive forgiveness of sins, and inheritance among them which are sanctified by faith that is in me.*

When the man and woman ate, their eyes did not become open. They became closed. Otherwise, why would it be necessary for the Lord to open our eyes? Only God is capable of properly handling good and evil. If we attempt to do it, what we are saying in essence is that we have made ourselves God and no longer need His direction.

Is God Equally Good to All?

We have already seen that God has the sun to shine on everybody, and that He has the rain to fall on both the good and the evil. We have seen that God will even bless the unthankful and the evil. He's letting His goodness happen to all. When it rains, everybody gets wet. God is impartial in His benevolence to man. But if this is so, why does it appear at times that God is not equally good to everybody?

It is by faith that we receive from God. The Bible makes it clear that without faith it is impossible to please God (Hebrews 11:6) and that we have all been given the same measure of faith (Romans 12:3). However, there are two variables involved in this equation. First, not everyone chooses to develop and use their faith; and second, we are all uniquely gifted and called.

Every vessel is not the same! There are different vessels in the house of God. There's that diversity again! Be satisfied that you are a unique and special vessel, and quit being concerned about the size and shape of everyone else. If you are a vessel, and if your vessel is full, then you should be content and ask the Lord for more to do! If we ever learn this truth, we can cut down on a lot of the condemnation that results when everyone doesn't receive the same things at the same time from God.

We're dealing with some heavy issues here. We have people telling us, "Look at me! Look at me!" And that might be the worst thing we could ever do. The Bible tells us again and again, "Keep your eyes on Jesus!" He made the vessels diverse from one another, according to His desire. He's given us different callings, which will require different gifts, different amounts of money, and different relationships.

The Goodness of God

God is working in us a thing that mankind cannot understand. God glories in diversity. We cannot understand that. Instead, we adopt an assembly-line mentality. We want every car to look the same. We want every boat to look the same. We want to be so alike! But learn this truth: We are *not* alike. God is a God who gives talents according to the way He has designed the receptacle. Even if we "containers" were exactly alike, we would not be the same because none of us has the same abilities.

That's why a choir must deal with sopranos, altos, tenors, basses, and baritones...and even some "in-betweens!" Not every one of the voices in a choir is exactly alike. Not every singer has the same level of ability. Yet we shouldn't become upset. We must use what we have! We each stand responsible before God for how we use what we have received from Him.

God doesn't want us all to be identical. If He did, He would have made us that way. No, God wants to show that He can bring forth His plan for mankind with diversity. He doesn't have to make everybody the same in order to accomplish what He set out to do. In fact, it appears that God thrives on the diversity of His people. Everybody doesn't talk the same! Everybody doesn't preach the same! Everybody doesn't sing the same! Everybody doesn't look the same!

Why? Because we are not the same! Therefore, God's goodness is portioned out in different ways to us as individuals, because we are not alike. We are not identical in our abilities. God wants us to stir up the gift He has placed in us (2 Timothy 1:6), not try to be someone else!

Even though some have received more of God's goodness than others, note this: God never withholds the necessities of life from anyone who trusts Him for them. My favorite passage in Psalm 84 says, *For the Lord God is a sun and shield: the Lord will give grace and glory: no good thing will he withhold from them that walk uprightly* (v. 11). No, God never withholds the necessities of life from those who trust Him.

However, I believe that God may bestow greater measures of His goodness upon those who, in turn, use it to bless others. Maybe some of us don't have as much as others because we don't use it correctly!

Consider the parable of the ten talents in Matthew, chapter 25. The man who had received just one talent was afraid to use it, and buried it. In the end, he even lost that to the others who had used the talents their Lord had given them. Jesus says to all of us that *if* we are faithful over the little He gives us, *then* He will make us rulers over much more. Are you asking for five talents when you haven't even used one yet?

Many times when God asks you to use what you have for His glory, it's not just for your own benefit, but also for the benefit of others. I believe when Paul taught the Corinthians about the gift of tongues and interpretation, he was making the point that operating in that gift was for the profit of the entire church. If you are using that gift to glorify yourself, you are not using it correctly.

The gifts of tongues and interpretation of tongues are given to the Church so we all might understand the message of God. I don't think these chapters in 1Corinthians concerning spiritual gifts are just for our inspiration. I believe they are for our correction. Paul is correcting the church of many problems, including the misuse of spiritual gifts.

How does this relate to the message of God's goodness? I stated that God does not withhold the necessities of life from anyone who trusts Him for them. I believe God bestows a greater measure of His goodness upon those who will, in turn, use it to bless others. Spiritual gifts are given to bless others as well as ourselves.

I further believe God might withhold some things from those who despise His goodness. Remember, Psalm 84:11 says, *No good thing will he withhold from them that walk uprightly.* What about those who despise God's goodness? Is He still obligated to bless these individuals? Well, I've got Scripture to cover this question: *Therefore thou art inexcusable, O man, whosoever thou art that judgest: for wherein thou judgest another, thou condemnest thyself; for thou that judgest doest the same things. But we are sure that the judgment of God is according to truth against them which commit such things. And thinkest thou this, O man, that judgest them which do such things, and doest the same, that thou shalt escape the judgment of God? Or despisest thou the riches of his goodness and forbearance and longsuffering; not knowing that the goodness of God leadeth thee to repentance?* (Romans 2:1-4.) God very clearly states that if you despise the riches of His goodness, He'll hold them back from you.

What about churches that refuse to allow the gifts of the Spirit to operate? I believe the gifts don't operate because the gifts are not desired. God told us to desire the spiritual gifts (1 Corinthians 14:1). Yet many churches say, "We won't have these things here under any circumstances!"

Now let's go back to the parable of the talents. What happened to the man who refused to use his one talent? He despised God's goodness. He hid it. "Oh, no, I couldn't use it, Lord! I was afraid!" How did Jesus respond? "Hey, you despised the riches of My goodness!" And He took from him the one talent he had received and gave it to the one who loved the goodness of God the most.

In Romans, chapter 2, Jesus warns us not to despise the riches of His goodness. Maybe that's why some folks aren't getting what they ought to get. Maybe it's not a lack of faith. Maybe it's not a lack of holiness or sanctification. Maybe it's despising God's goodness.

Consider again Psalm 84:11: *No good thing will he withhold from them that walk uprightly.* What about those who do not walk uprightly? They place themselves in the wrong place at the wrong time, and they are not in position to receive all God wants them to have. Consequently, He can share their blessings with someone else who is walking uprightly and in a position to be blessed.

Just think about the position we put ourselves in when we despise God's goodness! Then we get angry because we think God is using someone else more than He is using us. We sit back, thinking we're so spiritual but wondering why nothing exotic is happening in our lives in relation to God. We sit there and say, "I'm still waiting for my change to come!"

Well, I've got news for you! We're not getting any change! If we don't have anything to give, we can't get change from zero! If we bring zero, what kind of change do we expect to get?

Do not Despise God's Goodness

Some of us have stayed in a miserable rut for years because we have despised the riches of God's goodness. We have seen God be real good to some folks and have become very upset. We set ourselves apart, not realizing that we're actually despising the goodness God has shown to our brothers and sisters.

Instead of viewing those who have received God's goodness with contempt, jealously, and envy, we should be rejoicing with them and encouraging one another. Instead of saying, "Well, what does she think she's doing?" we should be saying, "Go ahead, girl!"

Then there are those who have a very high opinion of how they have worked and studied to succeed in life and provide for their families. They make light of God's goodness. There is nothing wrong with working hard—it's a godly trait—but any time a person thinks he's doing it on his own, he's despising God's goodness.

Depending too much upon ourselves and our own abilities is a dangerous snare. God said, *O taste and see that the Lord is good: blessed is the man that trusteth in him* (Psalm 34:8). We'd better be asking God every day, "Show me the way! I don't know what's happening out here!"

Sooner or later, all those who have the idea that what they have is due to their own efforts and abilities and not to God's goodness can expect a great fall! Proverbs 16:18 tells us that pride will eventually bring destruction into our lives.

Having a high IQ is a blessing from God, but for some people, IQ means "I quit!...It's too tough for me! I give up! I can't handle it!" And that's what's happening with a lot of intellectuals in today's world. They're burning out and falling out because they are trying to do everything apart from God. We must use our intellectual abilities, but not overuse them by thinking the reason for our success is our own ability and not the riches of God's goodness.

Most people have not learned to comprehend that the goodness of God will lead them to repent of their pride and forsake their sins, which will in turn cause them to trust God for the daily supply of His goodness. Then they can *taste and see that the Lord is good.* His goodness is what leads us to trust in Him. He says, "Daily I will bless you with My goodness. I have riches of goodness!"

But we must learn this in our hearts. We must learn, as David did, how to bless God in our hearts. We must learn to say, *Blessed be the God and Father of our Lord Jesus Christ, who hath blessed us with all spiritual blessings in heavenly places in Christ* (Ephesians 1:3). We need to learn to say, *Thou art good, and doest good; teach me thy statutes* (Psalm 119:68).

Sometimes we look at our lives and think things aren't going too well. Well, that's our perspective, not God's. We don't know the final end of things. Psalm 119:71 says, *It is good for me that I have been afflicted; that I might learn thy statutes.* What is the psalmist saying? If we don't learn to thank God for His goodness, He will allow us to be in a position where we will be forced to learn. We might not like that verse, but there it is! I believe if we have verse 68 in operation in our lives, we won't have to deal with verse 71!

Now let's look at another scripture along this line—Psalm 86:1-7: *Bow down thine ear, O Lord, hear me: for I am poor and needy. Preserve my soul; for I am holy: O thou my God, save thy servant that trusteth in thee. Be merciful unto me, O Lord: for I cry unto thee daily. Rejoice the soul of thy servant: for unto thee, O Lord, do I lift up my soul. For thou, Lord, art good, and ready to forgive; and plenteous in mercy unto all them that call upon thee. Give ear, O Lord, unto my prayer; and attend to the voice of my supplications. In the day of my trouble I will call upon thee: for thou wilt answer me.*

This is a prayer! In our prayers, we are to praise God as the psalmist did. This type of prayer is called a *midal* prayer. God is thrilled by our *midal* prayers! He is thrilled when we tell Him how great He is. Some of us are that way too. Those of us who are great athletes, for example, thrive on comments like, "You're great, man!" We do our best to be humble, but we thrive on this adulation. But only God truly deserves it. He loves to hear our praises.

Now let's look at Psalm 106:1,2: *Praise ye the Lord. O give thanks unto the Lord; for he is good: for his mercy endureth for ever. Who can utter the mighty acts of the Lord? who can shew forth all his praise?* Hey, God is good! Once we have tasted and seen that goodness, we can't help but praise Him for it. And if we walk uprightly before Him, He will abundantly supply us with all of His goodness. He's rich in goodness. He's good ALL the time. One of God's great attributes is His goodness. And what makes it so beautiful is that He shares His goodness with everybody.

Take a good look at Psalm 107:1: *O give thanks unto the Lord, for he is good: for his mercy endureth for ever.* Again the psalmist is telling us about the first great attribute of God that was revealed to mankind—His goodness. The first thing we learned about God from the point of creation was that He is good. Everything He did was good. He is abundant in His goodness. He is greatly good. He's rich in goodness, and He is good to all mankind.

Chapter 7

Thanksgiving and the Goodness of God

Bless the Lord, O my soul: and all that is within me, bless his holy name.
—Psalm 103:1

Have you ever just stopped to think about all the blessings God bestows on you? Sometimes we need to just stop and say, "Thank You, Lord, for getting me up this morning. Thank You for blessing me this day!" We need to remember to thank Him for our food. In fact, we should thank Him for everything.

I remember an uncle of mine. He was my mother's brother and we always called him Uncle Bear. I was a grown man before I ever knew his real name. In fact, I didn't find out until the man died that his name was Henry—Henry Langston.

One thing I did know about Uncle Bear was that he loved chicken and dumplings. He'd come for a visit and Mama would cook his favorite dish, and I would watch him eat. First he'd take off his shoes. And when he dipped into those chicken and dumplings, he began to pat his feet and hum and eat...all at the same time! He loved those chicken and dumplings!

Hey, that's the way we should love the Lord! Sometimes we should just kick off our shoes and say, "God, You're so good to me! Yes, sir, like chicken and dumplings!" We need to bless Him with our whole heart, like the psalmist did. We need to bless Him with our soul!

Bless the Lord, O my soul, and forget not all his benefits: Who forgiveth all thine iniquities; who healeth all thy diseases. Who redeemeth thy life from destruction; who crowneth thee with lovingkindness and tender mercies; Who satisfieth thy mouth with good things; so that thy youth is renewed like the eagle's (Psalm 103:2-5). What are His benefits? It's His *agathos*...His goodness...His character ...His constitution that is beneficial in its effect! His hand that is extended to fill you with His goodness is a benefit. His goodness will encompass you everywhere you go. His goodness is present to deliver you from the presence of your enemies and even to prepare a table for you right before them. (See Psalm 23:5.) His goodness is a great benefit to you!

Notice Psalm 103:3: *Who forgiveth all thine iniquities; who healeth all thy diseases.* You must have forgiveness in order to get the benefit of His healing! He says, "I'm going to heal you, but you must go and sin no more!" God says, "I've got some good news for you! I've got a benefit for you! I can heal all of you!"

I like verse 4 so much that I quote it every morning: *Who redeemeth thy life from destruction!* That's good! You'd better remember that! *Who crowneth thee with lovingkindness and tender mercies!* Sometimes when I'm in my car on the freeway I turn on the radio and hear an accident report. "Both drivers are fatally injured," the announcer will say. No, they're not "fatally injured!" They're dead. You'd better hear it right. What kind of news is that? Both drivers are dead, but they say it real easy so you'll keep on driving without getting too upset. But God says, "My goodness is surrounding you. It's encamped around you because I'm a Spirit. I'm not limited. I can ride with you on those freeways!"

I like verse 5, too. It says, *Who satisfieth thy mouth with good things; so that thy youth is renewed like the eagle's.* In order to understand this verse, you need to understand something about eagles. The first thing I learned is that eagles don't flap their wings much when they fly. Their wing span is too large. Most often when an eagle flies, he soars! Therefore, the eagle always finds where the wind is blowing and rides the wind. Now *wind* in the Bible makes reference to the Holy Spirit. That's why the eagle doesn't have to worry.

The eagle might say, "I've got problems down here on the lower level." Then God says, "Get on the wind and come up higher!" When the eagle soars, he can get so high up there in the wind with God that the Grand Canyon looks like a tiny crack in the ground. So when you have a problem that appears to be so big, just soar upon the wings of an eagle and then look down at your problem from God's point of view. You'll see the goodness of God as He takes that mountain of a problem and makes it look like a molehill.

He'll renew you like the eagle. And because eagles are able to go up high, God will say to you, "Get on top of that mountain, boy!"

These are just some of the benefits of God. We could go on and on with Psalm 103, but the point is we should all develop the habit of blessing and praising God. Thankfulness is an important part of our Christian walk. We should give thanks for everything, from our food, to our jobs, to the homes we live in. All these things are demonstrations of God's goodness to us.

Why We Bless our Food
The Bible teaches that we should always bless our food, regardless of where we are, whether at home or in public. This is nothing new to those of us who have been trained to bless our food before we eat. But I would like to elaborate on this topic from the standpoint of the goodness of God. Why? Because although we have been trained to bless our food, some of us don't really understand its importance and significance. Yes, we bless our food before we eat, but why do we do it? Many of us don't have any idea. We just pray a quick prayer and dig in! It's almost like a ritual!

How does God respond to that? More importantly, how do we want Him to respond? To discover the answers, we need to first see some things about the goodness of God that are resident in His creation.

We must realize that all that emanates from God is good. It is good because God is essentially good. Therefore, every act of creation was an impartation of God's goodness. When God created us, He created us because He is GOOD! Those of us who are born-again believers, however, are *new creations* in Him. In other words, we are both natural creations and supernatural creations. When we were born again, we received an impartation of His goodness.

But nothing forced God to create mankind or the world. Did you know that God created the world and all that is in it—including you and me—because He *wanted to*? There were no demands placed upon God to create this world, yet He chose to do it. And because His nature is essentially good, He chose to create *all things* GOOD. So the first thing we should learn about God's creation—especially if His creation is an image or a reflection of who He is—is that it is GOOD. How do we know? Because the book of Genesis records that every time God stood back to survey the things He created, He observed, *It was GOOD!*

God wants us to know He is good. He told us of His goodness from the very beginning. All that He has created is good. Thus, God wants us to be recipients of His goodness. That fact is apparent from the very beginning of life on earth.

Another thing God wants us to know is that He is sovereign. Sovereign! It's time for the Church to bring back this dimension of the understanding of God, because men today actually think they are God. They are trying to do what God does. But they'll never do it! They're messing up real bad!

Only God is sovereign. And His goodness is a result of His sovereignty. You see, God's goodness has nothing to do with you! Even during times when you're out of the perfect will of God, His goodness is still right there. I heard a preacher remark once that he stayed in the doghouse with God so much that when somebody knocked, he didn't know whether to bark or shake their hand! Doghouse or no doghouse, God has never withdrawn His goodness, and He never will!

The sovereignty of God is expressed first in His creation, and is demonstrated by the expression of good. Most of us have not yet grasped the fact that God seeks to do *only good*! We need to really understand that, because if we don't watch out, we'll let Satan trick us! Yes, that's right! It's not God who is seeking to play tricks on us. God doesn't play tricks! He's only looking to do good. And one of the good things God promises to do for us is feed us.

Now, if He's going to feed us, don't you think we'd better be thanking Him for the food? When we humbly and gratefully offer thanks to God at the table for the food He has provided, that food actually acquires something. There is a spiritual transaction that takes place.

That's what Paul was telling us in Romans, chapter 14. When we set our food aside and sanctify it with prayer at the table, that food acquires a holy quality simply by our acknowledging that it is a gift from God. What, then, is the most important reason that we pray? To sanctify our food!

People in biblical times took praying over their food seriously. *As soon as ye be come into the city, ye shall straightway find him, before he go up to the high place to eat: for the people will not eat until he come, because he doth bless the sacrifice; and afterwards they eat that be bidden* (1 Samuel 9:13). This passage is saying, "We're not going to eat a thing until the man comes and blesses it! We want the holy attribute placed upon it."

Food Provides Strength

In Acts, chapter 27, Paul and his companions had been fasting. Paul broke his fast and instructed the others on board ship with him to eat also because the Lord had warned him they were about to shipwreck. *And while the day was coming on, Paul besought them all to take meat, saying, This day is the fourteenth day that ye have tarried and continued fasting, having taken nothing. Wherefore I pray you to take some meat: for this is for your health: for there shall not an hair fall from the head of any of you. And when he had thus spoken, he took bread, and gave thanks to God in presence of them all: and when he had broken it, he began to eat. Then were they all of good cheer, and they also took some meat* (Acts 27:33-36).

In the presence of everyone, Paul prayed. He gave thanks to God for the food they were about to eat. He was saying, "Do you know what's about to happen to us? We're about to have a shipwreck. This ship is going to crack up and break into pieces, but all of us are going to get safely to land. I'm going to pray to the God who is able to protect and keep us. And I want everybody else on board to know about Him too!"

Miracles, Loaves, and Fishes

As we read in Matthew, chapter 14, the story of Jesus feeding a multitude with a few loaves and fishes, we immediately see that food took on a different quality when Jesus prayed. *And he commanded the multitude to sit down on the grass, and took the five loaves, and the two fishes, and looking up to heaven, he blessed, and brake, and gave the loaves to his disciples, and the disciples to the multitude. And they did all eat, and were filled: and they took up of the fragments that remained twelve baskets full* (vv. 19,20). Jesus was saying, "Father, I want to use what You have provided for a holy thing, and I want a holy quality to be ascribed to this. I've got to do something above and beyond the normal task, and this little bit of food that I have here won't even help Me." Then He performed a miracle.

You see, in those days, a loaf of bread was not the size it is today. It was small like a biscuit. You could probably gobble up one of those loaves in about two bites. That was a humble little meal. But there were 5,000 people to feed! In order to feed all those people from just a few loaves and fishes, the food had to take on a holy quality. Even God in the flesh understood that. But He knew that if God, the Creator of all things, got involved, something would happen to the food.

So what did Jesus do first? He looked *up to heaven* [and] *he blessed* [it] (v. 19). He said, "Father, You're so good! Everything You create is good! These loaves and fishes are good! They were provided for the sustenance of human life. I'm out here preaching and doing what You told Me to do on earth, and I've got these hungry folks sitting here. How can I tell them about a superspiritual life when they can't even make it through the day in the natural life? All we have are five loaves and two fishes, but I'm looking up to the Creator of all! I'm going to call on Your first attribute—goodness!"

Then He looked up to heaven. Have you ever considered that, since He was God, He didn't have to do that? He was teaching you a lesson about thanksgiving and food. He was showing us that when we acknowledge God's gift of food, something is acquired. Even a little thing can be stretched into a big thing. Jesus said, "I'm sanctifying this food to You, Father, by word in prayer and faith. I'm thanking You. This is a gift from God! Now let it take on some holy qualities."

And I guarantee that only the involvement of God can stretch five loaves and two little fishes into enough food to feed thousands of people, with some left over! Actually, more than 5,000 folks were fed that day. How do I know this? The scripture says, *Five thousand men* (Matthew 14:21). Have you ever considered that each man probably also had an average of two children and a wife? That would be a total of about 15,000 to 20,000 folks! And that's just estimating that the men had an average of two children. Some of those families in Bible days had twelve or thirteen kids.

Jesus performed another miracle of multiplication in Matthew, chapter 15. Now, why did Jesus give us more than one account of this principle? So we'd know it can be done. This was no accident. Miracles like this can take place with the God we serve. And to prove it, Jesus was saying, "I'll do it again!" *And he took the seven loaves and the fishes, and gave thanks, and brake them, and gave to his disciples, and the disciples to the multitude. And they did all eat, and were filled: and they took up of the broken meat that was left seven baskets full* (Matthew 15:36,37). No, this was not an accident, nor was it a one-time-only miracle.

God's Goodness unto all Generations

The Lord bringeth the counsel of the heathen to nought: he maketh the devices of the people of none effect. The counsel of the Lord standeth for ever, the thoughts of his heart to all generations (Psalm 33:10,11). His heart is unto ALL generations! I like that! That includes MY generation. And that means, no matter how bad it gets out there, God is going to reveal Himself to us in this generation. And it might as well be you and me He uses to tell the world that God is good!

So you don't want to pray out loud in public? You don't want to pray over your food when you eat out in restaurants? You don't want the heathen to know you pray over your food? You'd better think about it. You should pray, and I don't mean just a quick, mumbled prayer. Close your eyes! Bow your head! You might even hear somebody say, "Look! He's praying over his food!"

Not only are you acknowledging that God is good by praying over your food and thanking Him that you have something to eat, but there's another important reason you should do it: You're getting ready to eat that! You need to sanctify it.

Blessed is the nation whose God is the Lord; and the people whom he hath chosen for his own inheritance. The Lord looketh from heaven; he beholdeth all the sons of men. From the place of his habitation he looketh upon all the inhabitants of the earth (Psalm 33:12-14). Another reason we should always pray over our food is that God sees! Just saying, "In God we trust" isn't enough. God has already told us how we can get out of the problems we're in. Now He's showing us that we can have an abundant supply.

Psalm 145:14,15 says, *The Lord upholdeth all that fall, and raiseth up all those that be bowed down. The eyes of all wait upon thee; and thou givest them their meat in due season.* In other words, God is saying, "You won't get anything unless I give it to you. You couldn't work if I didn't give you the strength. The man you work for couldn't pay you if I didn't give him the money. And he wouldn't even be in business if I didn't give him a business to run and supply the people to do business with."

Thou openest thine hand, and satisfiest the desire of every living thing (v. 16). Yes, He just opens His hand! *The Lord is righteous in all his ways, and holy in all his works. The Lord is nigh unto all them that call upon him, to all that call upon him in truth. He will fulfil the desire of them that fear him: he also will hear their cry, and will save them. The Lord preserveth all them that love him: but all the wicked will he destroy* (vv. 17-20). The key here is that God says, "I'm going to do something for My people." What is He going to do? He's going to do GOOD to them!

Unthankfulness: A Slap in God's Face

Unthankfulness is nothing more than a slap in the face of God's goodness. When a man or a woman takes the necessities of life for granted and does not express their thankfulness to God, it's a slap in His face. Just think about that. God said throughout the book of Genesis, "Everything I created is good. I created it for you, and you ought to be appreciative of My goodness." *And God saw every thing that he had made, and, behold, it was very good* (Genesis 1:31).

God wants us to notice something, so He says, "Behold! Have you learned anything yet? Have you seen that all I've created is good, and that I'm really good? Have you beheld this truth yet?" But notice something else about verse 31. In this verse God did not simply say, *It was good.* He said, *It was VERY good!*

Just consider all the people who presume upon God. They use all of His blessings, and then throw them away. They misuse and abuse His goodness by never once saying, "Thank You!"

Then, in these last days in particular, there are those telling us what kind of diet we should be on, and what kinds of food we should eat. But let's see what the Bible says about these end-time health fanatics. The Apostle Paul wrote in 1 Timothy 4:1-3: *Now the Spirit speaketh expressly, that in the latter times some shall depart from the faith, giving heed to seducing spirits, and doctrines of devils; speaking lies in hypocrisy; having their conscience seared with a hot iron; forbidding to marry, and commanding to abstain from meats, which God hath created to be received with thanksgiving of them which believe and know the truth.*

Paul is saying, "I don't know about these guys who command that you abstain from certain foods. These guys are going by some strange spirits! But I do know one thing. God created all foods to be received with thanksgiving!" Why does Paul say all things were created to be received with thanksgiving *of them which believe and know the truth?* Because you must believe and know!

Then Paul says, "Now, let me tell you something. For every creature (the Greek translation says, 'For every created thing') is good." We've seen the goodness of God reflected in His creation. We've seen the attributes of God in His creation, and that it's all good. Therefore, nothing is to be refused.

But I'd like to add that what you eat is a matter of choice, because you can't eat everything. None of us is capable of eating all there is to eat. If something gives you indigestion or high blood pressure, leave it alone! But if we want to have pork chops now and then, and it won't make us sick, it's all right. Nothing is to be refused IF it is *received with thanksgiving: For it is sanctified by the word of God and prayer* (1 Timothy 4:4,5).

And the Bible also tells us to use moderation and good sense. God said, "Now, all of this that I've created is good!" But too much of anything is not good! Remember when your mother used to dole out the sweets and each child got one cookie? "One cookie? That's not fair!" So you tried to sneak another one! The worst problem about food in the Church is not what we eat, but how much of it we eat!

Peter's Powerful Vision

In Acts 11:5-10 Peter writes: *I was in the city of Joppa praying: and in a trance I saw a vision, A certain vessel descend, as it had been a great sheet, let down from heaven by four corners; and it came even to me: Upon the which when I had fastened mine eyes, I considered, and saw fourfooted beasts of the earth, and wild beasts, and creeping things, and fowls of the air. And I heard a voice saying unto me, Arise, Peter; slay and eat. But I said, Not so, Lord: for nothing common or unclean hath at any time entered into my mouth. But the voice answered me again from heaven, What God hath cleansed, that call not thou common. And this was done three times: and all were drawn up again into heaven.* In this passage, God tells us again that all things are good for us to eat. Now, this might seem to be a small thing to learn, but this vision was given to Peter, a Jew who observed the Jewish laws concerning food.

Believe me, if you're eating out in restaurants, the greatest thing you can learn about this passage in Acts is that God cleanses our food when we pray. You don't know what's behind those swinging doors of that restaurant! All you know is that somebody comes to your table with a pad and pencil, takes your order, then disappears. Then all of a sudden, those swinging doors open up again, and here comes your food. The waiter brings it to your table and says, "Enjoy!" But you don't have any idea who prepared that food or how clean the kitchen is.

Notice that God told Peter, *Slay and eat.* Consider that when you think about the various groups today who say you should not eat meat. They eat nothing but leaves, grains, and herbs. And I'm not knocking that. But as for me...give me some meat! Besides, you don't SLAY leaves! God didn't say to Peter, "Go saw down a tree!" He said, "Slay!"

You can eat some herbs. Herbs are good. But Genesis, chapter 1, reveals God's original dietary plan for mankind. Although He mentions herbs, notice there are

The Goodness of God

some "ands" in there...*and fowl that may fly above the earth* (v. 20)...*and beast of the earth* (v. 24). All food is good. It's the sustenance of life. And we should thank Him daily for all these good things.

Notice that Acts 11:10 says, *And this was done three times.* God emphasized three times the statement, *What God hath cleansed, that call not thou common* (v. 9). That's three witnesses—Hebraic proof that you can trust! God is saying, "If I cleaned it, it's clean, and don't you call it anything else!"

Now let's look at two verses from Romans, chapter 14. *I know, and am persuaded by the Lord Jesus, that there is nothing unclean of itself: but to him that esteemeth any thing to be unclean, to him it is unclean* (v. 14)...*For meat destroy not the work of God. All things indeed are pure; but it is evil for that man who eateth with offence* (v. 20). Verse 20 does not refer to food in general—it's about meat!

You see, some folks out there are saying, "Don't you dare eat pork!" Paul said there would be folks like these in the last days. You might call them the "non-pig-eating" group!

Then there are those who say, "Don't you dare eat eggs!" Some people eat eggs and live long lives, and some people don't eat eggs and die. What's going on? You can live in that sterile environment if you want to miss out on some of the goodness of life, but I can tell you this: You're going to die some day anyway—oh, yes you are—unless Jesus comes before then!

I'm not saying we shouldn't watch our diets. But there's a word here that I think is really the bottom line: moderation! Moderation is the key. God is the giver of all foods, and all foods were created by Him to be good. When we give thanks for our food, we are responding to that goodness and acknowledging that God is the giver of what we eat.

The Substance of Life

Why does He give us food? Because food is *the sustenance of human life!* Food also brings enjoyment. Come on, admit it! Sometimes we eat for pure enjoyment. Most of us eat when we aren't even hungry. Sometimes we eat because we don't have anything else to do. Sometimes we eat in response to television advertisements, and we suddenly find ourselves saying, "Yeah! I wonder what's in the refrigerator?"

But basically, food is for our sustenance. In other words, as we eat food, God is saying, "I am even helping you to perform the tasks you need to perform for Me. I give you strength so you can continue to put food on your table. I'm giving you energy! I'm giving you intellectual power. Food is doing something for your brain so you can think straight. It's giving power to your body so you can work that job." It's God working in you. Just to be able to do the normal things in life is deliverance. It's health!

Full of God's Riches

Listen to what the psalmist says: *O Lord, how manifold are thy works! in wisdom hast thou made them all: the earth is full of thy riches* (Psalm 104:24). He says all of God's works are good. And all of His riches are good. And He makes all those things available to me. So, in a sense, I'm rich! Every time I eat, I sit down to the richness of God, even if my meal is nothing but a hot dog.

God wants us to behold this. He's saying, "Don't presume on Me!" Just think about that! Not only did God make the heaven and the earth, but He made you and me and said, *It is God which worketh in you both to will and to*

The Goodness of God

do of his good pleasure (Philippians 2:13). In this verse, He is saying, "I want to do something good *for* you, something good *to* you, and something good *with* you!" But He is also saying, "Even though I'm good and all that I do is good, don't presume on Me!" Psalm 119:68 says: *Thou art good, and doest good; teach me thy statutes.* The psalmist concludes in simple terms that God is good! He's saying, "Everywhere I go...everywhere I look...everything I do...everything I have is because Thou art good!" That's a good thing to be aware of.

What else is the psalmist saying in this verse? He is telling us that God *doest good.* Because He IS that way, He ACTS that way. He IS good, so He DOES good. The psalmist is saying, "Since You're so good, there is only one thing I need from You now. *Teach me thy statutes!* Just teach me about Your goodness, because I want to taste of Your goodness. And if I *taste* it, I'll find out something!" *O taste and see that the Lord is good: blessed is the man that TRUSTETH in him* (Psalm 34:8; emphasis mine)! Why? Because as we taste, our TRUST increases.

Taste...and you can expect something to happen. Expect it! And the more you taste, the more blessed you'll be because you will have seen that God is good.

The repetition of spiritual tasting is what builds up your trust in God. Perhaps you've been given all kinds of "steps" to go through to increase your trust in God—one, two, three, four...a, b, c, and d! Do you want to be a strong person in God? *Taste! See* how good God is! Seeing His goodness will lead to a greater trust in Him, and that greater trust will lead you into the abundance of His blessings.

Then you'll be able to say with the psalmist, *Thou art good, and doest good; teach me thy statutes* (Psalm 119:68).

Then you'll be able to *taste and see that the Lord is good* (Psalm 34:8)!

"O Give Thanks!"

First Chronicles 16:34 says, *O give thanks unto the Lord; for he is good; for his mercy endureth for ever.* You'll find that same statement in Psalm 106:1, and again in Psalm 107:1 and Psalm 136:1.

Now let's go to 2 Chronicles 5:13,14: *It came even to pass, as the trumpeters and singers were as one, to make one sound to be heard in praising and thanking the Lord; and when they lifted up their voice with the trumpets and cymbals and instruments of musick, and praised the Lord, saying, For he is good; for his mercy endureth for ever: that then the house was filled with a cloud, even the house of the Lord; So that the priests could not stand to minister by reason of the cloud: for the glory of the Lord had filled the house of God.*

Throughout the Old Testament, as we've seen, the refrain resounds, *O praise the Lord, for he is good; for his mercy endureth for ever!*

The books of Chronicles were the Old Testament newspapers of biblical times. And in those newspapers, the people were told repeatedly, "The Lord is good! Praise Him!" Too bad our modern-day newspapers don't print the same thing. Instead, they put stories of brutal killings on page one and bury the story about the lady who gave a large sum of money back on page 20 somewhere. The headlines for good news aren't as catchy, it seems.

Let's look at the people's response to God's goodness reported in 2 Chronicles 7:3,4: *And when all the children of Israel saw how the fire came down, and the glory of the Lord upon the house, they bowed themselves with their*

The Goodness of God

faces to the ground upon the pavement, and worshipped, and praised the Lord, saying, For he is good; for his mercy endureth for ever. Then the king and all the people offered sacrifices before the Lord.

We find a similar report in Jeremiah 33:11: *The voice of joy, and the voice of gladness, the voice of the bridegroom, and the voice of the bride, the voice of them that shall say, Praise the Lord of hosts: for the Lord is good; for his mercy endureth for ever: and of them that shall bring the sacrifice of praise into the house of the Lord. For I will cause to return the captivity of the land, as at the first, saith the Lord.* Again God is saying, "I'm helping My folks all the time! Why? Because I'm good!"

O taste and see that the Lord is good: blessed is the man that trusteth in him (Psalm 34:8).

Now let's go to Psalm 118, where we will see the goodness of God displayed yet again: *O give thanks unto the Lord; for he is good: because his mercy endureth for ever...I called upon the Lord in distress: the Lord answered me, and set me in a large place. The Lord is on my side; I will not fear: what can man do unto me? The Lord taketh my part with them that help me: therefore shall I see my desire upon them that hate me. It is better to trust in the Lord than to put confidence in man. It is better to trust in the Lord than to put confidence in princes* (vv. 1,5-9).

It's always good to have somebody on your side. *The Lord is on my side; I will not fear: what can man do unto me?* (v. 6). *O taste and see that the Lord is good: blessed is the man that trusteth in him* (Psalm 34:8). What are you trusting in—Pennsylvania Avenue? Washington, D.C.? Only trusting God will bring the blessing. He says, "You just call upon Me...I'll help you!"

What's the Problem?

By now you probably won't deny that God is good. You've seen too many scriptures that reveal His goodness. You have *tasted!* You have *seen!* But I would like to point out, in closing, where I believe people most often miss it with God. The problem is we don't praise Him. That's where we make our mistake. We don't praise God for His goodness.

Some of us don't even praise Him for our food. We just sit down and dig right in without first thanking God and asking for His blessing. We go to work and forget to thank God for the jobs we have. Then we wonder why our names are on the list when it's time to get laid off. All of a sudden we're in distress!

But even in distress, we have discovered that God is good. Remember the many distresses in your life? God helped you even when you were in distress. And He will still work for you. *Oh that men would praise the Lord for his goodness, and for his wonderful works to the children of men* (Psalm 107:15,21,31)!

But do thou for me, O God the Lord, for thy name's sake: because thy mercy is good, deliver thou me (Psalm 109:21). How do we know His mercy is good? It *endureth for ever!* That's how we know!

Now look at Psalm 135:2-6: *Ye that stand in the house of the Lord, in the courts of the house of our God, praise the Lord; for the Lord is good: sing praises unto his name; for it is pleasant. For the Lord hath chosen Jacob unto himself, and Israel for his peculiar treasure. For I know that the Lord is great, and that our Lord is above all gods. Whatsoever the Lord pleased, that did he in heaven, and in earth, in the seas, and all deep places.* Did you hear that? God has CHOSEN you! You are His *peculiar treasure.* You know how you protect your own treasures—your minks and jewelry. You hide them. You keep them safe. You say, "Hey, don't mess with my mink!" Well, that's the way God is about YOU! He says, "Handle with care! That's my treasure! That's mine!"

We must understand that we mean something to God. And if He shows His goodness to the children of men, how much more will He show it to those of us who are His *peculiar treasure!*

Whatsoever the Lord pleased, that did he in heaven, and in earth, in the seas, and all deep places (Psalm 135:6). I like that! God can do what He wants to do. It pleased God to show His goodness to us in heaven, in earth, and even in the seas. It means that even in the storms of life, God will help us when we are in trouble. That's the bottom line.

Psalm 9:11-14 says: *Sing praises to the Lord, which dwelleth in Zion: declare among the people his doings. When he maketh inquisition for blood, he remembereth them: he forgetteth not the cry of the humble. Have mercy upon me, O Lord; consider my trouble which I suffer of them that hate me, thou that liftest me up from the gates of death: that I may shew forth all thy praise in the gates of the daughter of Zion: I will rejoice in thy salvation.* I like that! In every situation, God hears the cry of the humble.

Again the problem is that many of us won't humble ourselves enough to realize that we are not man or woman enough to make it in this world. We've been trained to believe we can do it ourselves, on our own. We hear it from our parents, from our teachers, from our friends. But God said, "No, you *can't* do it!" And that's a hard thing to accept if you've been trained virtually your whole life to believe you can do it on your own. You're told, "You can do it! Just dedicate yourself. Put the effort out there! Do it!" Then God comes along and says, "Give it up. Trust Me. Lay it on Me. You *can't* do it!"

Still we try to prove we can do it, and all we're doing is messing up. That's the problem! We've been trained to be so independent that when it's time to become dependent on God, we resist. We don't want to humble ourselves. For some reason, humility has been taken off the list of desirable characteristics in a person. We interpret humility as meaning we are less than we should be. But in God's view, it's the place where we all should be. *Humble yourselves therefore under the mighty hand of God, that he may exalt you in due time* (1 Peter 5:6). We must humble ourselves!

Remember, O Lord, thy tender mercies and thy lovingkindnesses; for they have been ever of old. Remember not the sins of my youth, nor my transgressions: according to thy mercy remember thou me for thy goodness' sake, O Lord. Good and upright is the Lord: therefore will he teach sinners in the way (Psalm 25:6-8). Yes, sir! I've prayed that prayer before! And I didn't even know that it was in the Book, but there it is! *Good and upright is the Lord!* Now we can see why the psalmist says, *O taste and see that the Lord is good: blessed is the man that trusteth in him* (Psalm 34:8).

Deliverance...help...and all of God's goodness is available to the man or the woman who will *taste and see* and discover for themselves how good God really is. *Taste and see!* You'll never experience Him for yourself unless you *taste and see* that the Lord is good! May God richly bless you as you *taste and see!*

Epilogue

I hope you have received benefit from this "excursion" into the goodness of God. If you are a born-again believer, I pray this message will enhance your practical experience with God and help you in your Christian walk.

If you have not been born again, I would like to pray for you:

> *Father, I pray for this man or woman who has not been born again. Enlighten them. Let them know that goodness is not possible to attain within themselves, but that it must come from Jesus Christ, who is the fullness of Your goodness. Each of us must pursue Him, for if we fail to pursue Him, there is Your severity. I pray that no one will be dealt with in Your severity, but that all will come to Christ. I pray for those today who would like to realign their lives with Christ. Help them start anew, walking in Your goodness and allowing Your goodness to be demonstrated in them. Let every man and every woman know that today is the day to make their decision for Christ! In Jesus' name, Amen.*

I encourage you to make that most important decision now. It will affect not only how you live the remainder of your life on earth, but it will determine where you will spend eternity. If you would like to receive Christ right now, please pray with me:

> *Father, as a sinner, I come to You now. I confess my sins and ask You to forgive me. I repent, turn from my sins, and decide to follow You. I acknowledge that Christ died for my sins and rose again on the third day. Jesus, I accept You as my Lord and Saviour. Teach me Your statutes. Reveal to me Your goodness and help me to demonstrate that goodness each day as I live my life for You. In Jesus' name, I pray. Amen.*

God bless you!

About the Author

Dr. Edward L. Haygood, B.A., M.A., Ph.D., is the founder and pastor of Agape Christian Fellowship, serving the southern area of Los Angeles, California. The Agape ministry was formed in 1980.

Dr. Haygood is gifted in expository teaching, focusing on basic Bible truths and explaining the rich meanings of the Bible's original Greek and Hebrew words. In addition to teaching the Word of God to his congregation, he ministers as a guest speaker at churches and various ministries throughout the Los Angeles metropolitan area, including effective outreaches to foreign students and prison ministries.

Dr. Haygood received his Ph.D. in Bible Exposition in 1978 from the California Graduate School of Theology. His Masters Degree in Health and Safety Education was awarded in 1971 by California State University at Los Angeles, and his Bachelor of Arts Degree in Special Education was completed in 1960 at San Jose State University.

Author of two other books, *Why the Tithe?* and *What Makes Christmas Special?* Dr. Haygood's favorite Bible verse is Hebrews 11:6—*But without faith it is impossible to please him.*